THE INDIVIDUAL AND HIS RELIGION

THE INDIVIDUAL
and
HIS RELIGION

A Psychological Interpretation

by GORDON W. ALLPORT

THE MACMILLAN COMPANY, NEW YORK

COLLIER-MACMILLAN LIMITED, LONDON

150726

TO
ADA

CONTENTS

PREFACE

EVER SO MANY PEOPLE at the present time find themselves interested in both psychology and religion. Psychology is a solidly growing science: there is hope that it may emerge as the decisive science of the twentieth century. It is also currently fashionable—perhaps too much so for its own good. While popular interest in psychology mounts, religion remains as ever one of the prominent concerns of mankind. This concern has existed since the dawn of history—probably long before—and has not been diminished by the social and moral catastrophes of the past three decades. Those who are interested in both psychological science and religion are quite naturally asking what the two subjects have to do with each other. Both seem so intimately tied to the future destiny of the human race.

As every reader knows, modern empirical psychology initially separated itself sharply from religion. "Psychology without a soul" became its badge of distinction and of pride. There was good reason. Too long had the understanding and cure of man's spirit been regarded solely as the province of religion and philosophy. In order to bring to bear the demonstrated merit of the scientific method and inductive thinking psychologists were forced to chart a new course. Turning their backs upon the altars of religion and forsaking the philosopher's armchair they adopted the methods of the laboratory and clinic. Their reward came promptly in the accumulation of verifiable facts and in a growing area of agreement with fellow scientists. If the agreement was not perfect it at least surpassed by far the agreements previously reached by religionists and by philosophers. Since the progress and prestige of psychology depend upon its preserving a strictly scientific orientation there is no prospect—unless an authoritarian darkness should engulf the world—that the historical separation of inductive psychology from deductive ideology, whether philosophical, political, or religious, will end.

At the same time there is inherent absurdity in supposing that psychology and religion, both dealing with the outward reaching of man's mind, must be permanently and hopelessly at odds. As different as are science and art in their axioms and methods they have learned to co-operate in a thousand ways—in the production of finer dwellings, music, clothing, design. Why should not science and religion, likewise differing in axioms and method, yet co-operate in the production of an improved human character without which all other human gains are tragic loss? From many sides today comes the demand that religion and psychology busy themselves in finding a common ground for uniting their efforts for human welfare.

It is my belief that before such a harmony of effort can arise the parties of both parts will need a greater flexibility of outlook than they customarily display. A narrowly conceived science can never do business with a narrowly conceived religion. Only when both parties broaden their perspective will the way to understanding and co-operation open.

In these pages I have not concerned myself with possible programs of joined effort (excepting in Chapter Four where I examine the respective roles of psychology and religion in advancing mental health). Rather have I undertaken the task that has logical precedence, namely the task of discovering the place of religion in the life-economy of the individual. For without a psychological understanding of the nature and functioning of the religious sentiment all talk of mutual policy on the one hand, or of "opiates" and "superstition" on the other, is prejudiced or empty.

My effort, as I say, is directed solely to a portrayal of the place of subjective religion in the structure of personality whenever and wherever religion has such a place. My approach is psychological, some would call it naturalistic. I make no assumptions and no denials regarding the claims of revealed religion. Writing as a scientist I am not entitled to do either.

In defining my approach as psychological I do not mean to imply that every psychologist would agree with the analyses I make. Although psychology is certainly a science, it is not yet a unified science. There are many self-consistent frames of psychological interpretation, each covering the facts available. Whether in the distant future, when many more experiments and observations have accumulated, it will be possible to impose a univocal set of interpretations upon all human conduct, we cannot yet say. Many think such a unified science will come to pass. Others believe that the explanations of mental life will always be subject to philosophical disagreements. I do not pretend to know the answer to this riddle, but offer my own interpretations in the light of what I understand to be the most acceptable tenets of modern dynamic psychology.

The system of dynamic concepts upon which my analyses rest is set forth in my book *Personality: A Psychological Interpretation* (1937). In one sense the present volume may be viewed as a specialized expansion of this earlier work. But, unless I err, the concepts I employ and the basic conclusions I reach are in line with much of the advanced thinking in modern psychotherapy, in phenomenology, in neo-Freudianism, and in other departments of current psychological research and theory. Whether a given representative of these schools will accept in every detail my account of subjective religion I cannot, of course, predict.

One underlying value judgment flavors my writing. It is a value that to my mind every supporter of democracy must hold: the right of each individual to work out his own philosophy of life, to find his personal niche in creation, as best he can. His freedom to do so will be greater if he sees clearly the forces of culture and conformity that invite him to be content with a merely second-hand, and therefore for him, with an immature religion. It is equally essential to his freedom of choice that he understand the pressures of scorn and intimidation that tend to discourage his religious quest altogether. Such pressures emanate from narrowly conceived science, and from some teachers and writers who, in the face of the bigger issues of life, are as ignorant and helpless as any other seeker.

Critics may complain that I have divided my attention somewhat unevenly between these two obstacles to freedom of choice. Perhaps I have said less about the operation of second-hand, authoritarian, and immature religion in personality than I should. On all sides we see how bigotry and escapism accompany certain forms of piety. One travels through America and notes its Jim Crow churches, its storefront tabernacles, its anti-Semitic "Christian" crusaders, and marks how often the darkness of the human mind is sanctified with a religion of superstition. Religion in many lives seems merely symptomatic of fear and frustration.

My reason for not dwelling more fully than I do upon the

function religion plays in infantile and neurotic personalities is that I am seeking to trace the full course of religious development in the normally mature and productive personality. I am dealing with the psychology, not with the psychopathology, of religion. The neurotic function of religious belief, its aid as an "escape from freedom," is indeed commonly encountered, so commonly that opponents of religion see only this function and declare it to dominate any life that harbors a religious sentiment. With this view I disagree. Many personalities attain a religious view of life without suffering arrested development and without self-deception. Indeed it is by virtue of their religious outlook upon life—expanding as experience expands—that they are able to build and maintain a mature and well-integrated edifice of personality. The conclusions they reach and the sentiments they hold are various, as unique as is personality itself.

William James perceived this point when fifty years ago he wrote his incomparable *Varieties of Religious Experience*. I should not presume to restate his thesis if I did not feel that the progress of dynamic psychology in the past two generations has been great enough to warrant its sharpening and reinforcement. James did not have access to modern theories of personality. It is a tribute to his genius that in most respects these theories readily accommodate his earlier findings and interpretations.

These chapters represent a revision of the Lowell Lectures delivered by me in Boston during the spring of 1947. They were read in their present form as the Merrick Lectures at Ohio Wesleyan University in the spring of 1949. I am grateful to the trustees of both foundations for providing the incentive and opportunity to formulate my thoughts on the subject.

I have been fortunate in my critics and helpers. In many ways I have depended upon Mrs. Jacqueline Sutton and Mr.

James Gillespie, especially in connection with the research reported in Chapter Two, and upon the constant assistance of Mrs. Eleanor Sprague. Dr. Seward Hiltner, a shrewd student of the psychology of religion, has given me many helpful suggestions and strategic encouragement. Generous aid came likewise from Professor Edgar S. Brightman of Boston University and from Swami Akhilananda, of the Church of the Vedanta in Boston. The former strove to keep me from undue psychocentricism, and the latter from ethnocentricism. Professor Peter Bertocci of Boston University was a vital source of encouragement and in a friendly way endeavored to repair my inexpertness in dealing with certain philosophical and theological issues.

The combined efforts of these kindly critics have not fully corrected my failings; for in an area as large as religion, and so extensively studied, a psychologist is an intruder. Theologians, philosophers, religious workers, historians, have long had prior rights. It is impossible to treat the subject, even from the limited psychological point of view, without trespassing upon their territory. At the same time the psychologist—this psychologist at any rate—cannot forever keep silent. He too has something to say. Specifically he wishes to be heard on the function of the religious sentiment in the personality of the individual.

GORDON W. ALLPORT

March 21, 1949

THE INDIVIDUAL AND HIS RELIGION

Origins of the Religious Quest

AMONG MODERN INTELLECTUALS—especially in the universities—the subject of religion seems to have gone into hiding. Is it because the educated portion of mankind is learning to live with less finality and is coming to distrust embracing formulae of all types? Or is it because in their zeal to liquidate pseudo-knowledge and to discover truth in a piecemeal fashion the universities have found it necessary quietly to adopt a thoroughgoing secularism? Whatever the reason may be, the persistence of religion in the modern world appears as an embarrassment to the scholars of today. Even psychologists, to whom presumably nothing of human concern is alien, are likely to retire into themselves when the subject is broached.

During the past fifty years religion and sex seem to have reversed their positions. Writing in the Victorian age William James could bring himself to devote barely two pages to the role of sex in human life which he labeled euphemistically the "instinct of love." Yet no taboos held him back from directing the torrent of his genius into the *Varieties of Religious Experience*. On religion he spoke freely and with unexcelled brilliance. Today, by contrast, psychologists write with the frankness of Freud or Kinsey on the sexual passions of mankind, but blush and grow silent when the religious passions come into view. Scarcely any modern textbook writers in psychology devote as much as two shamefaced pages to the subject—even though religion, like sex, is an almost universal interest of the human race.[1]

It is not difficult to understand the reluctance of psychologists to enter a field that is both technical and tortuous, where institutional interests and historical considerations are of overpowering concern, and where methods of psychological research are few and undependable. It requires a certain hardiness of spirit for a psychologist to pronounce upon a subject that involves so many departments of life, and to which he brings little in the way of special research or knowledge.

Yet he has no right to retire from the field. Fully two-thirds of the adults in our country regard themselves as religious people, and at least nine-tenths, by their own report, believe in God.[2] A sentiment and a belief of such extent cannot be disregarded whether for reasons of professional modesty or disinterest. What is more, at just this juncture of the world's history literate people are growing more and more concerned with the relation between psychology and religion.[3] Perhaps the reason is that while the majority subscribe to the tenets of an historic faith they find that they hold the faith with many mental reservations. Why, they

[1] A detailed analysis of the treatment of religion in currently used textbooks is to be found in *College Reading and Religion*, New Haven: Yale University Press, 1948. Chapter 3 deals with the place accorded to religion in modern textbooks of psychology.

[2] The evidence for these estimates is diverse but fairly secure. See *Opinion News*, April 15, 1948, Chicago: National Opinion Research Center; G. W. Allport, J. M. Gillespie, J. Young, The religion of the post-war college student, *Journal of Psychology*, 1948, 25, 3–33.

[3] One sign of the times is the enormous popularity of a book that attempts to fuse psychiatry and religion: Rabbi Liebman's *Peace of Mind*, New York: Simon and Schuster, 1946.

wonder, do doubts increasingly haunt them? They note too that, while they still "feel" religious, the regulative principles for their conduct are coming less and less from their religious belief and more and more from psychology, psychiatry, and mental hygiene.

This trend toward doubt, toward secularism, toward psychologism, does not in the slightest degree mean that religion is a thing of the past, or that it is on the way out. History shows that as fast as institutional religion decays it has a way of reviving. The nineteenth century, marked as it was by increasing secularism, none the less witnessed the Oxford Movement, the Evangelical Revival, the birth of Christian Science, and the founding of the Salvation Army. The present century has seen the further spread of these movements and the resurgence of many fundamentalist sects, as well as a striking growth of ecumenicism. But it is not with the condition of organized religion that we are concerned.

The argument of this chapter is that the subjective (personal) religious sentiments of mankind—whatever the fate of institutional religion may be—are very much alive and will perhaps always remain alive, for their roots are many and deep.

Is There a Single Form of the Religious Sentiment?

Before we ask about the roots of religion in the life of the individual we do well to inquire whether there is a single basic form of experience that is inevitably a part of every religious sentiment.

It would be convenient if we could discover such a common denominator for the religious sentiment. Many attempts have been made to do so. One of the best known of these is Schleiermacher's. This writer claims that the distinctively

religious experience is a "feeling of absolute dependence."
In the last analysis religion is a sense of appeal, dependence,
surrender. Many subsequent writers have been fascinated by
Schleiermacher's attempt to find one central and distinctive
attribute in the religious sentiment. But each has preferred
his own version of the case.

Rudolf Otto felt that Schleiermacher had overlooked the
cognitive counterpart of dependence. After all, the individual,
overwhelmed by his own nothingness, is yet aware of a
mysterious reality, "tremendous and fascinating," on which
he is dependent—a reality "wholly other" than man himself.
The intention of the Sanctus in the Mass would, to Otto,
represent the quintessence of religion. *Holy, Holy, Holy* is the
heart of all religion. Since no other aspect of human experience entails this "amazement absolute," the religious sentiment, Otto concludes, is basically unique and unlike any
other human experience.[4]

But even while we are admiring Otto's analysis we turn to
Wobbermin and discover that to his mind the feeling of
security and the sense of longing are insufficiently represented
in either Schleiermacher or Otto. The psalms and prayers
in all religious cultures, he insists, are replete with references
to both longing and security. In Buddhism, for example, the
feeling of dependence, so central to Schleiermacher's analysis,
recedes while the feeling of security and poignant longing
are dominant.[5]

I shall not multiply examples, for this type of analysis,

[4] Friedrich Schleiermacher's argument for the autonomy of the
religious sentiment is contained in his *Addresses on Religion to Its
Cultured Despisers*. Rudolf Otto's famous work, to which, of course,
my brief digest does scant justice, is *The Idea of the Holy*, Oxford:
University Press, transl. 1923. An excellent secondary survey of the
subject is contained in R. F. Davidson's *Rudolf Otto's Interpretation
of Religion*, Princeton: University Press, 1947.

[5] G. Wobbermin. *The Nature of Religion*, New York: Thomas Y.
Crowell, transl. 1933, Chapter 6.

however gratifying to the individual author, is foredoomed to failure. Each analyst seems to pinch a bit here and pull a bit there, in order that the formula for subjective religion may include his own introspections. Writers of this type are essentially autobiographical and unconsciously project their own delicate states of religious sensitivity upon all mankind. It is important to reject this approach at the outset, for if the religious sentiment were of uniform composition, marked by a single phenomenal core, then our task of psychological analysis would be straightforward; but if this simplicist approach is not acceptable—and it is not—then our attack must be pluralistic and varied.

Most psychologists who have written on religion seem agreed that there is no single and unique religious emotion, but rather a widely divergent set of experiences that may be focused upon a religious object. It is the habitual and intentional focusing of experience rather than the character of the experience itself that marks the existence of a religious sentiment. The wide variety of emotions that may enter into the religious intention is depicted by James:

There is religious fear, religious love, religious awe, religious joy, and so forth. But religious love is only man's natural emotion of love directed to a religious object; religious fear is only the ordinary fear of commerce, so to speak, the common quaking in the human breast, in so far as the notion of divine retribution may arouse it; religious awe is the same organic thrill which we feel in a forest at twilight, or in a mountain gorge; only this time it comes over us at the thought of our supernatural relations; and similarly of all the various sentiments which may be called into play in the lives of religious persons.[6]

Dunlap denies both a unique or universal religious emotion and likewise the existence of universal religious concepts.

[6] William James. *Varieties of Religious Experience*, 1902. Modern Library Edit., p. 28. By permission of Longmans, Green & Co.

Although historical religions, he finds, frequently deal with certain common concepts, they do not invariably do so. Interest in divinities generally exists, though not universally. Daimons, spirits, and souls are commonly but not always a matter of concern. Problems of cosmology and metamorphosis are usually present, but there may be exceptions. Sin, salvation, and life after death are topics of only frequent interest. Mystical states and the idea of holiness are usually, but not invariably, included. In dealing with this core of conceptual interests, which is only approximately common, the individual himself experiences an infinite variety of mental states. There are "no feelings and no emotions that are not experienced by devotees of one religion or another; and in most of the religions of the world the whole gamut of feelings and emotions is involved, each emotion or feeling being experienced in appropriate circumstances."[7]

True, James and Dunlap are somewhat extreme in their pluralism. Many authors prefer to establish a fixed norm for the religious sentiment and then to admit, a bit grudgingly, that individual variations do occur. One recent writer, Max Schoen, goes so far as to speak of the religious experience as "subject to a variety of distortions."[8] It seems odd for a psychologist to speak of "distortions of experience." An experience is what you have. While it may conceivably distort reality, it can scarcely distort itself. The error of Schoen, and of the majority of writers on religion in its subjective aspects, is that they do not refer the task of characterizing the religious consciousness to the only authorities capable of knowing what it is—namely the individuals who experience it.

In denying that the religious pattern in the individual's life

[7] From *Religion: Its Function in Human Life* by K. Dunlap. 1946. Courtesy of McGraw-Hill Book Co.

[8] Max Schoen. *Thinking about Religion*, New York: Philosophical Library, 1946, p. 12.

possesses a standard form, we are not thereby denying it a personal form. Quite the contrary, in any given individual there are characteristic feelings and recurrent concepts highly typical of his own mental life. He is likely to have a well-organized personal sentiment that can presumably, with intensive psychological study, be accurately construed and understood. Even though in their religious lives people are not consistent with one another, they are as a rule markedly consistent with themselves.

Is There a Common Origin of the Religious Sentiment?

Just as there is no standard pattern of content in subjective religious experience, so too there is no common point of origin. To deny the existence of a single religious *instinct* entails no heresy in modern psychology, for it would be difficult to find any writer who makes a case for such an instinct. Even McDougall, the arch instinctivist of the present century, found no evidence for a single underlying religious propensity. Rather, he considered the emotion of reverence to be very complex. Into it enters awe which itself is a blend of *fear* and *admiration*. Admiration, in turn, represents a fusion of *negative self-feeling* and *wonder*. In addition, reverence includes *gratitude*, a binary compound of the *tender emotion* and *negative self-feeling*. Underlying this emotional complex at least four McDougallian propensities are at work: curiosity, self-abasement, flight, and the parental instinct.[9]

Though we fail to find psychological support for a single and specific religious instinct we do find a tendency to identify religious thought and feeling with the operation of some one single bodily or mental mechanism. The theory of sex repres-

[9] W. McDougall. *Outline of Psychology*, New York: Charles Scribners' Sons, 1923, p. 334.

sion, for example, has its devotees. For evidence they cite the prominence of sex symbols in religion and the orgiastic nature of some forms of religious frenzy and mystical fantasy.[10] Religion, they maintain, is a thinly veiled sublimation of the aim-inhibited sexual impulse. But this line of reasoning overlooks the even greater emphasis that religion gives to symbols of nutrition, security, repose. It is likewise specifically guilty of confusing all forms of excitement with sex emotion, or else of darkening counsel by equating sex with completeness. In any case it overlooks the passionlessness that marks so much of religion. Also, we know, religion flourishes over the face of the earth in places and in epochs that know no sex repression. If further refutation be needed, we have reports from present-day youth. Given a free and anonymous opportunity to comment on this subject, only 8 per cent of 500 students recently interrogated thought sex turmoil was a factor in their religious awakening, while 23 per cent mentioned gratitude, 17 per cent sorrow and bereavement, and 42 per cent fear and insecurity.[11]

As if to discredit the evidence of such introspective reports another simple and sovereign correlate of the religious life has been advanced, namely, the alleged operation of the "unconscious." If the roots of religion lie wholly below the threshold of awareness, then, of course, introspection is valueless. The famous exponent of this view is Freud who maintains that the individual's conception of God "is in every case modeled after the father." Our personal relation to God is dependent upon our relation to our physical parent. "God is at bottom nothing but an exalted father."[12] If true, the

[10] Cf. James H. Leuba. *The Psychology of Religious Mysticism*, New York: Harcourt Brace, 1925; and Theodore Schroeder. "The erotogenesis of religion," *The Alienist and Neurologist*, 1913, 34, 3–25.

[11] See Chapter Two, p. 39.

[12] Sigmund Freud. *Totem and Taboo*, New York: Moffat, Yard and Company (translated by A. A. Brill), 1918, p. 242.

correctness of this statement depends upon the existence of deeply repressed, infantile ideas which, Freud thinks, strive to express themselves whenever the individual finds life rough going.

There are many other ways in which religion has been tied to the unconscious. William James, for example, invoked the hypothesis of a subliminal connection between the individual's mind and a universal mind. The island of individual consciousness, to use his analogy, rests ultimately upon the limitless ocean floor from which it draws its composition and support. The theory that the individual mind is merely a fragment of a universal mind is common in many religions as diverse in type as Hinduism and Christian Science. To some extent this theory seems to be present in nearly every religion. Its merit, as James himself clearly saw, is metaphysical rather than psychological. It provides a possible channel for the inrush of divine consciousness into the individual mind.

Psychologically, any theory of unconscious origins is difficult to prove or to disprove. The only thing we can be sure of is that such theories are one-sided. The force of the unconscious cannot be the whole story, for a large array of conscious causal forces lie also at hand.

Perhaps the most striking fact about subjective religion is the contrast between its essential simplicity when, well-formed, it is playing its part in the economy of the personal life, and its extreme complexity in the process of forming. It is a rich pudding, smooth and simple in its blend, but intricate in ingredients. Or, to dignify the metaphor, it is a white light in personality which, though luminous and simple, is in reality multicolored in composition.

To make a spectroscopic analysis is not easy, since the prisms of each personality are unique. In nearly all instances, however, we find that in the course of development the religion of the individual has been refracted by (1) his bodily needs, (2) his temperament and mental capacity, (3) his psychogenic interests and values, (4) his pursuit of rational explanation, and (5) his response to the surrounding culture. Each of these formative factors requires separate comment, although it is only through their synthesis that they engender the religious sentiment.

The Role of Organic Desire

All of human life revolves around desire. And, as Dunlap says, "there seem to be no desires that are not, or have not at some time been, items in religions. Prayer certainly is an expression of desire, and there is nothing which man could desire that some man does not or has not prayed for."[13]

Among the basic desires of men are those pertaining to food, water, and shelter. Fear, too, is an early and important ingredient in the individual and in the race. Man's life, bracketed between two oblivions, is haunted by fear—of enemies, of nature, of sickness, poverty, ostracism; most of all of death, for of all creatures on earth man alone knows that he will die. Do we invoke the protection of an amulet, do we trust ourselves to the everlasting arms, do we discipline ourselves to seek Nirvana and so escape the threats that hover over us? To demand some form of reassurance is a spontaneous response to insecurity. The typical religious supplication results, with variants in all faiths:

> Guidé me, O thou great Jehovah,
> Pilgrim through this barren land.
> I am weak but thou art mighty,
> Hold me with thy powerful hand.

The reciprocal of fear is the desire for companionship. In most human beings the capacity to love is great and the desire

[13] Dunlap. *Op. cit.*, p. 126.

for love insatiable. It is doubtful whether even the happiest of earthly lovers ever feel that they love or are loved enough. A margin of yearning remains. And if death takes the beloved from this world, the desire mounts. A small child in her bereavement nightly addressed her prayers to her dead mother. Culture did not sanction this practice; it was not taught by her elders. Rather it was for her a spontaneous solution of an insupportable conflict. Her religion was nourished by her orphan hunger.

Customarily it is in the critical periods of life, when desire is more intense, that religious consciousness is acute. Many people are religious only in moments of crisis; the rest of the time they rub along comfortably and godlessly, content to let their religious sentiment lie dormant. But it is important to note that what is felt as a crisis by one person is often not so regarded by another. One young girl became devout in the course of praying that her parents might not obtain a divorce, another in her desire to be delivered from haunting nightmares. Bereavement or self-reproach often engender vivid religious experience. The longing for a suitable marriage may lead the Catholic maiden to say a Novena for divine assistance. Over and over again in a multitude of ways, the religion of the individual brings to a focus the mingled motives and desires of an unfulfilled life.

It is unnecessary to exhaust the list of contributing desires. Their multiplicity is indicated by the varying conceptions of deity held by different individuals and by one and the same individual at different periods of time. Sometimes the attribute of power is stressed; God is omnipotent—the creator and able to still the tempests; the heavens declare His glory. Sometimes He is the source of security and strength, an ever-present help in time of trouble. Often He is cosmic perfection, to be worshiped in the beauty of holiness. When we need affection, God is love, knowledge, He is omniscient; consolation, He granteth peace that passeth understanding.

When we have sinned, He is the Redeemer; when we need guidance, the Holy Spirit. Divine attributes plainly conform to the panorama of desire, although the individual is seldom aware that his approach to his deity is determined by his present needs.

An interesting rite in the Hindu religion here comes to mind. Around the age of sixteen or eighteen, the Hindu youth receives from his teacher a name for God which all his life long shall serve this youth as a private instrument for prayer and for binding himself to the deity. In this custom Hinduism recognizes that the temperament, needs, and capacities of the initiate himself must in large part determine his approach to religious verities. A young person with an unusually affectionate nature will seek in God the complement to his love. Hence the name "Beloved" may be privately assigned to him. A theoretically minded youth may be advised to select *Soham*, a name that affirms the unity of all existence. In preparation for this rite the teacher assumes the responsibility for correctly assessing the personality of his charge. Although other religions provide personal counsel for the initiate at the threshold of maturity, probably none goes to such lengths in making a close analysis of the youthful personality. In this practice we have a rare instance of an institutional religion recognizing the ultimate individuality of the religious sentiment. The fact that the teacher takes upon himself more responsibility than a psychodiagnostician in the West would like to assume is not here the issue.

In India it is not enough that each individual should have a name for the deity suited to his own personal needs; it is also strictly advised that this name be kept secret even from one's bosom friends and from one's spouse. In the last analysis each person confronts his deity in solitude, and it is thought well to symbolize this fact, especially in overcrowded households and communities, with the seal of secrecy. It has been said that a congenial husband and wife, or two bosom friends, not infrequently have received identical names for God, thus signifying the astuteness of teachers in perceiving the likemindedness of two developing personalities. But so closely are the names guarded that the frequency of this occurrence cannot accurately be estimated.

Temperament

This Hindu rite clearly recognizes underlying differences in temperamental constitution. Some men live always close to the region of pain and melancholy; they are bound to emphasize the grimmer aspects of whatever they encounter, and to stain their religious sentiment with their sense of forlornness. Others have started in life with sparklets and bells; even in their moments of dependence they incline to take a sanguine view of the operations of Providence. Both the gloomy and the gay may be concerned with the wrongness of life and may seek a religious mode of righting it, but their paths will be separate. Their theological and ritualistic preferences will differ according to their emotional thresholds, according to the quality of their prevailing mood, and according to their tendency to express or to inhibit feeling. Moreover, they are likely to be sharply biased in favor of these preferences, and correspondingly critical of others who find a different sort of religion better adapted to their needs. In this obdurate fact of temperament there lies a practical limitation to the aspirations of the current ecumenical movement.[14]

[14] I do not mean, of course, that the ecumenical movement is foredoomed to failure. Roman Catholicism and Hinduism, both quasi-ecumenical, find place for a great variety of temperaments. But it is difficult to write a formula for church unity in advance that will adequately respect the varieties of temperament seeking satisfaction in organized religion.

The roots of religion that lie in temperament are but poorly understood. Indeed, the entire relation of genetics to the temperamental foundations of personality is still unexplored territory. The time is fast approaching, however, when psychologists who have banked so heavily upon the forces of the environment in fashioning personality will have to devote an equivalent amount of energy to the study of the inborn climate of personality. Until they do so, a false picture of human nature will prevail.[15]

Psychogenic Desires and Spiritual Values

I have suggested that subjective religion is, in the first instance, the flower of desire. Many desires, including those having to do with nourishment, rest, sex, and physical safety, are clearly organic in character. We share them with all animal life. For the most part these viscerogenic desires have a one-to-one correspondence with the tissue needs of the body. But there are other desires, psychogenic in character, that are very different from viscerogenic desires. We recognize the latter as subjective and private, and though they may indirectly nourish the religious hunger, especially when they are blocked, yet in themselves they normally clamor for objects which bring direct bodily satisfaction. Psychogenic desires, by contrast, are objectified. We long for information, let us say, and we locate the desired knowledge somewhere outside ourselves, calling it Truth. Or perhaps we long for fair and just social relations, and call them Good, again objectifying the value we seek. A symphony or a stained glass window furnishes satisfaction to our aesthetic hungers. Beauty

[15] William H. Sheldon's *Varieties of Human Temperament*, New York: Harper, 1942, is a book that somewhat alleviates our ignorance but at the same time makes us aware of the long road of research that lies ahead.

too we locate outside ourselves. The inner restlessness that seeks satisfactions of this order is more complex than the specifically localized, segmental drives of the body. It is also a distinctively human, as opposed to animal, motive.

Now anything that yields a satisfaction or provides a means for such satisfaction we designate a "value." Chronologically the viscerogenic or "bodily" values precede the psychogenic or "spiritual" values. Further, all values grow ever more generalized. The infant, who at first merely "consumes" one concrete value after another as they are successively presented to him, soon comes to recognize food, companionship, playthings, as broad categories of desiderata. Similarly in the psychogenic realm, not only does some particular act of justice yield satisfaction but it does so for the reason that it conforms to an abstracted class of activities that constitute our sense of what is good and right. Gradually then we come to regard Goodness, Beauty, Truth, Holiness as categorical. They exist outside ourselves, in some realm of essences, and determine the objects toward which much of our striving is directed. Not all psychogenic interests are socially or spiritually desirable. There are hungers for self-expression, for adventure, for power, which, I believe, are properly classed as psychogenic, but these are readily recognized as being relatively self-centered and not so widely removed from the viscerogenic drives in which they originated.

To illustrate the evolution of values and their final bearing upon subjective religion, let us take the central phenomenon of egoism. The infant, so far as we can tell, is not at all self-conscious. He reacts to stimuli, expresses his wants, consumes the satisfaction offered, and lapses into quiescence. Philosophically we are probably required to attribute to the infant from birth, if not before, the possession of a self; but with almost perfect assurance we can assert that only in the second year of life does he commence to relate his experiences to himself and begin to act as a reflexly conscious agent. Only when he comes to resent offenses against his person, encroachments upon his dignity, is he building up a sense of his own ego as an object of value. This stage in a child's development, marked, as it usually is, by stubbornness and negativism, is unmistakable. From the age of two onward the most universal of all values resides in the keen sense of individuality which constantly demands self-expression, craves power, and feels pride. Our organisms are so constructed that our personal life is the highest value that we ever know directly. Yet by indirect stages the evolution of this value continues much further.

Soon I come to ask myself, "If I am acutely self-conscious and disposed to brook no less majesty against my person, are not others, in all probability, equally attached to their egos?" And thus abstracting from my physical individuality the general concept of selfhood, I gradually come to value whatever makes for the conservation of personal integrity anywhere. The Natural Rights of Man, the Golden Rule, the Second Commandment of Christ, are varied statements of the value that I affirm. I affirm it because in the course of my own development the generalizing powers of my mind have brought my own sense of selfhood into higher combinations. Where once only my personal life was the supreme value, I now acknowledge the worth of *any* person. And this enlarged value may come to subsume, depending on my own trends of logic and the teaching offered me, many subordinate values such as charity, tolerance, equality. My concept of the person may by now be even divested of corporeal attributes without thereby losing its insistent character. God Himself I may declare to be the supreme expression of personality, a necessary and final value *required* to explain and to conserve all other values of selfhood.

This psychogenic interest in the integrity of personality beginning with my own ego, and developing finally to embrace both an ethics and a theology, is only one illustration of the process I am depicting. The world of art, the world of science, as well as the social universe around us, are all concerned with the production of values capable both of satisfying us and enlarging our horizon. We become eager that no value should perish. God as Beauty would guarantee the conservation of the values in art; God as Truth would assure them to science and philosophy; God as Love would conserve all that strikes us as valid and worth preserving in human relations; God as Infinite would establish the interconnectedness of values in all these realms. It is this line of thought that led Höffding to declare all religion to be motivated by the individual's desire to conserve value.[16] What he will wish to conserve depends upon his own needs, and needs vary from individual to individual, from nation to nation, and from time to time. When values do not rise above the egoistic level, the resulting religion is designed to conserve self-interest; when they are more highly abstracted and generalized, as in the affirmation of the worth of personality, the character of the religious faith broadens. Höffding notes further that it is when values come into conflict with the struggle for existence that subjective religion is most acutely felt, for when values are threatened a conserving agent is most needed. Thus it comes about that under conditions of fear, illness, bereavement, guilt, deprivation, insecurity, the restoration of values through religion is commonly sought.

Pursuit of Meaning

Now the factors that we have been considering—desire, temperament, values—are relatively speaking the more emotional roots of the religious sentiment in the individual. It is

[16] Harald Höffding. *The Philosophy of Religion*, transl. B. E. Meyer, New York: Macmillan, 1906.

unfortunate that limitations of vocabulary force psychological analysis to treat emotion and reason, affection and cognition, as if they were separate provinces of mental life. From the point of view of the concrete functioning of the human mind nothing could be more false than is this division. In reality every emotional state is freighted with knowledge. Take two such elementary passions as terror and anger. The distinction between them, odd though it seems, is largely cognitive in character, for the bodily changes in both are virtually identical. In terror we know we are trapped; in anger we figure we have a fighting chance. Though the cognitive ingredients are swiftly and subtly marshaled, no emotion is devoid of them. Conversely, even our most crystal clear moments of logical reasoning would not take place at all unless they were sustained by present motivation (that is to say, by some state of desire).

It follows that subjective religion, like all normal sentiments, must be viewed as an indistinguishable blend of emotion and reason, of feeling and meaning. When we study it we are dealing with neither rationality nor irrationality, but rather with a posture of the mind in which emotion and logical thinking fuse. We are dealing with a mode of response wherein a combination of feelings is tied to a conception of the nature of things that is thought-provoking, reasonable, and acceptable. It is regrettable that we have no term in the lexicon of psychology to designate this cognitive-affective fusion. The only term that approximately fills our need, and the one we shall adopt, is "sentiment," though its flavor unfortunately suggests feeling more than meaning.

Because of this unbalanced connotation it is necessary to call special attention to the explanatory significance of the religious sentiment in the individual's life. He may, in a cool Thomistic manner, be able to demonstrate to himself the steps of proof for the existence of God, and continue, in the same fashion, to define the world in such a way that all his thoughts and feelings slip nicely into place. Under the guidance of such a sentiment, unifying feeling and meaning, his life proceeds fluently, and he experiences both ease and peace. All the great religions of the world supply, for those who can subscribe to their arguments and affirmations, a world-conception that has logical simplicity and serene majesty.

Most individuals, however, are not sufficiently contemplative nor sufficiently imitative to adopt in toto the explanation offered by any one master theologian. They may grasp parts of his system of thought, and sense the direction of the system as a whole. But they find that they require their own interpretations when they are in the grip of the engrossing pressures of their lives. In times of acute desire it is not the perfection of a system as a whole that satisfies but some aspect of it that renders intelligible and supportable the needs of the moment.

I am saying that all the while we are fretting, desiring, valuing, we are often busily seeking to interpret our own unrest. Early we come to realize that our frustrated longings are not in any literal or direct way satisfied through religion. Terrestrial food, drink, shelter are still necessary for survival; justice, beauty, truth, are still sought; but we do ask why we have such longing, what is the purpose of seeking its satisfaction? What is it all about anyhow? In many lives questions of this sort are remarkably insistent, and the curiosity they engender, like the clinging ivy, fiercely demands a support.

The universe is simply incomprehensible. Fragments of it may be fairly well understood, but not the interrelation of these fragments, and certainly not the design of the whole. Every man wonders at times about the void which gave way to creation, and about the successive links that connect this original void to his own momentary state of wonder. To many men, religion is primarily a search for complete knowledge, for unfissioned truth.

This appetite for meaning differs from person to person, and owing to nature's preference for diversity, some are satiated earlier than others. Furthermore, the capacities of individuals for comprehension differ, as do ability and inclination to make use of scientific explanations or of poetic metaphor. No two people have identical intellectual difficulties or powers, and hence no two reach identical solutions.

Is This Rationalizing Tendency Magical?

Some writers scoff at this rationalizing tendency in religious thinking, and regard it merely as a prelogical prelude to empirical and scientific thinking. This view was a favorite with certain older anthropologists who, possessing a handful of evidence from primitive tribes, argued that people who think religiously are, like primitives, living in a magical phase of development. The argument holds that we confuse the utilitarian and the sacred. Unable to control scientifically the propagation of plants, the navigation of ships, the construction of durable and effective tools and weapons, the primitive is said to have recourse to incantation, ritual, and prayer. Similarly in our own culture the child or the ignorant adult resorts to religious practices instead of adopting empirical procedures in order to solve his dilemma.

The error in this derivation of the religious sentiment is partly a mistake in fact and partly a mistake in interpretation. Pointing to the error in fact, Malinowski has shown that the Trobriand Islander, for example, possesses an impressive and accurate store of scientific knowledge that governs his fishing, gardening, and boat-construction. He is realistic and genuinely scientific in much of his thinking and behavior. It is true that, side by side with this severely empirical mode of thought, there exists a system of magical practices and beliefs, but these are specifically not confused with it.[17] The native knows full well that successful results will follow only from empirically proper manipulations. At the same time he knows there are factors in the situation beyond his rational understanding and control. For this reason he engages, just as do the majority of people the world over, in a dual set of expressions, the one to deal with factors within comprehension and control, the other with factors beyond comprehension and control.

Take the case of sickness and death. All people of all times have had scientific remedies to employ, medicinal herbs, techniques of first aid, therapeutic exercises. But they have also invoked religious aid. In our own culture the dual nature of these resources is clearly recognized. We know that when we summon a doctor and when we summon a priest we are acting on entirely different levels. Probably to the primitive the boundary is somewhat more obscure, and yet, according to Malinowski, he too is not unaware of transposing his problems to the religious plane.

The point is even more clearly brought out in bereavement. Probably no people on earth, primitive or civilized, believe that incantation, ritual, or prayer will resuscitate a corpse. Yet, as Parsons has pointed out, in no society does death lack ritual observances far in excess of the utilitarian need for disposing of the corpse and for making other practical adjustments. The strong emotions caused by bereavement have everywhere resulted in the development of religious ceremonies that are engaged in simply because minimal practical adjustments are felt to be inadequate. Thus, we cannot concede that funeral ceremonies, whether in the primitive or

[17] Bronislaw Malinowski. *Magic, Science and Religion and Other Essays,* Boston: Beacon Press, 1948.

in the civilized world, are the result merely of an unscientific view of death.[18]

If religious thinking were identical with prelogical thinking we could not account for many facts in the development of our own culture. History shows us that with relatively few exceptions religious institutions themselves have fostered the development of logic, mathematics, and scientific method. Church schools, with few exceptions, teach the same science as do private universities. And we could probably prove that throughout history those Christians who have accomplished the most practical benefit in this world are those who believed most fervently in the next.

The fact of the matter is that scientific thought is known by most people, primitive or civilized, to be able to cover only part of the ground. It goes a long way but not far enough. In Max Weber's terminology science deals with problems of empirical causation, religion with problems of adequate meaning. For most people, even for primitives, it is not hard to assign to science that which is science's and to religion that which is religion's. How the atomic energy of the sun reaches the earth or how it may be released through nuclear fission are problems of empirical causation. Problems of the creation, purpose, and ethical control of atomic energy are all of a different stripe. How a young child came to be burned to death is an empirical question that can be answered; why such things must happen is a question of a wholly different order.

The Bias of Intelligibility and the Bias of Optimism

For the most part the problems of meaning which people commonly refer to the religious mode of thought have to do

[18] Cf. Talcott Parsons. The theoretical development of the sociology of religion, *Journal of the History of Ideas*, 1944, 5, 176–190.

with the issue of creation or with the issue of evil. Cosmo-logical wonder is surely one of the commonest of all origins of religious thinking. "Where wast thou when I laid the foundations of the world?" the Lord asks of Job.

But even more insistent is preoccupation with evil, re-flected in the great literature of all religions. Typical are the opening pages of the Yogavasistha, a sacred Hindu text dating probably from the sixth century.[19]

What happiness can there be in the world where everyone is born to die? Everything comes into existence only to pass away. . . . Life is as evanescent as autumnal clouds, as the light of an oilless lamp, and as the ripples on the surface of water. . . . Desire is as fickle as a monkey. It is never satisfied with the objects already in hand, but jumps to other un-attained ones. . . . There is nothing good in the body. It is an abode of disease, a receptacle of all kinds of agonies, and subject to decay. . . . What delight can we have in the portion of our life called youth, which comes like a flash of lightning, soon to be inevitably followed by the thunder-claps and the agonies of old age? . . . What direction is there from which cries of suffering are not heard? . . . Let me know the best possible secret of becoming free from the suffer-ings of life.

Like many religious systems the Yogavasistha is intended for people who are keenly alive to the undesirable aspects of life and eager to know the secret of self-liberation.

The purpose of creation and evil are twin problems of meaning that have throughout the ages been referred to religious systems for their solution. In virtually every life these problems exist side by side, although it is quite cus-tomary for one individual to direct his quest more pointedly toward the solution of one of these problems than of the other.

To the extent that the individual finds some approximate or partial solution to these vexing problems, his whole life

[19] B. L. Atreya. The Yogavasistha and Its Philosophy, Benares: The Indian Bookshop, 1939 (rev. ed.).

is shifted in some degree toward intelligibility and optimism. Religious people are often heard to say, "I don't know what I would do without religion." This remark testifies to the relatively satisfying framework of meaning they have attained. To destroy such intelligibility and such optimism would be to cut much of the ground from under their existence.

Does this frequent bias of religion toward optimism, intelligibility, and the conservation of value indicate wishful thinking? Although the charge is commonly made, it is usually superficial. For one thing it overlooks the fact that the character of the hope and the tenor of the explanations involved in religion have very little to do with the clamorous wishes of ordinary life. What is demanded by the great religions is self-abnegation, discipline, surrender. To find one's life one must lose it. Such a transposition of values is too extensive to be covered by the formula of autism that is applied appropriately only to daydreams and to the rationalizations of daily life that are transparent in their self-centeredness. Only occasionally, I think, do we find individuals in whom religion runs its course on the level of wish-fulfilling fantasy. When this occurs we are dealing with a merely abortive religious sentiment in the individual.

The bias of intelligibility is by no means peculiar to the religious outlook on life. It saturates mental processes of all types. Take simple sensory perception, for example. As we let our eye wander about the room in which we sit, we conveniently overlook the sensory gaps that result from the blindspots in our retinas. When we read a page of proof we are satisfied with the meaning we derive that we may overlook many typographical errors. When we think of a race of people, perhaps with a feeling of dislike or hostility, we have created an inner world of meaning that finds little or no support in biological or anthropological fact. All our life is biased in the direction of obtaining simplified perceptions and categorical meanings. If we say that the intelligibilities of religious people leap far ahead of verifiable evidence, we must not forget that the intelligibilities of irreligious people do so likewise. All our cognitive operations press toward coherence and unity. Whether we be theists or atheists, we are prone to stereotype the world we live in.

Equally inevitable is our bias toward optimism. No young man, says G. B. Shaw, ever *really* believes that he is going to die. The doctor and his patient usually assume, and always act, as though health will result from the medical service. Yet a doctor who himself lived long enough would be bound to lose every one of his patients, and equally bound to suppress this certainty of defeat in favor of the optimistic bias. Most college students, we know, have a rosy and unreal view of the income they will earn after leaving college. But we regard this optimistic tendency as a wholesome mark of aspiration and legitimate ambition, and not as illusion, because after all there is a genuine element of uncertainty involved. All of us expect to be alive next year and yet actuarial estimates indicate that one and a half per cent of us will not be. Wherever there is uncertainty, hope springs eternal. The irreligious individual no less than the religious plans for a happy landing.

And so we see why it is unsound to trace the origin of the religious quest to the desire for escape from reality. It is true that religion tends to define reality as congenial to the powers and aspirations of the individual, but so too does any working principle that sustains human endeavor. Those who find the religious principle of life illusory would do well not to scrutinize their own working principles too closely.

Culture and Conformity

I have argued that desiring and valuing and the pursuit of meaning, conditioned by temperament and capacity, spin the threads that become woven into the subjective religious pattern, and that the infinite diversity of these threads guarantees that each weaver's design will be unique. But am I not in danger of overstating the case for pluralism? Must we not grant that culture imposes rigid constraints that tend to offset nature's preference for diversity? A child brought up in the Confucian tradition could not possibly arrive unaided at the intricate system of Christian theological beliefs held by many inhabitants of the Western world. And why throughout the ages has proselyting into far lands been necessary except to offset the strict cultural determination of religious belief?

Conformity to culture, especially during the period of childhood, is indeed an important origin of the religious quest. In all lands the social training of the child directs him to translate tribal ritual into personal habits. At first the religious practices prescribed for the young child have no meaning for him, at least none of the meaning that they will later come to have. He regards the ritual as something that his group (his family or his tribe) engages in, and learns that to perform the required act is to cement his identification with those who provide him security, affection, approval. The fast of Ramadan, the prayers of the rosary, grace at table, a silent Quaker meeting—a child ordinarily learns to participate in these rites before he learns the corresponding myth that explains their purpose. And when the myth is learned it too is at first accepted without question for the same reason the ritual was adopted. The in-group is safe and familiar and therefore whatever it does and says is good and right.

We accept this interpretation offered us by cultural anthropology, and we accept likewise three additional facts of importance taught by this discipline. First, the cultures of all peoples in the world give great prominence to ritual and myth, and all possess some mode of organization or priesthood to sustain religious beliefs and practice. Secondly, wherever religious systems are hopelessly disrupted, the consequences for the life of the people are disastrous, unless some equivalent systems of belief replace them. Thirdly, religious systems are not independent of the remaining portions of a culture, but are intimately integrated with them. For this reason the supplanting of one religion by another is not possible unless the culture itself is basically altered. The threads of religion are lockstitched into the social and economic fabric. Agricultural peoples worship deities of fruition. In India the caste system has been closely bound to the belief in the transmigration of souls; for if one's deeds in a previous existence are responsible for the state of one's life in this world, there is little point in protesting against one's present placement in a caste. And our own Protestantism, as Max Weber makes us see, is inextricably related to the rise of capitalism in the West. Whether we could have had one without the other is doubtful.

In view of all these indisputable ties between religion and culture would it not be wise to define the former in terms of the latter? Should we not say that religion is merely a culturally created design for living, acting as a potential guide for the behavior of men? That its utility within the culture guarantees that it will be handed on from father to son? And that the child believes what he believes because he was taught to believe it?

Many social scientists are content with this type of analysis, but it is far too gross. For one thing it assumes that the religious sentiment of an individual is a faithful replica of the cultural model that is offered him. We can put this assumption to a test very easily by asking ourselves whether our religious views do in fact mirror faithfully those of our parents, teachers, or clergy. There would be few affirmative answers to this question. How then does it come about that so many individuals within a culture fail to reflect the systems of belief that were carefully taught them?

The reason is that the place of religion in the personal

life is basically different from its place in society. The social scientist argues that the function of religion is to produce social stability. Yet no individual, I venture to assert, is religious for any such reason. Indeed, most people would hasten to discard their religion if they thought it was merely a device to keep them out of the hands of the police and out of their neighbor's hair. Further, the social scientist tells us that religion is a culturally sanctioned vent for the release of overstrong emotions which would be disruptive if expressed in society. But from the individual's point of view strong emotions are only rarely involved in his religious life, and their social control is a matter of no particular concern to him.

It is certainly true that rulers in all ages have enjoined religious faith and observance upon their subjects in order to secure social stability and prevent untimely outbursts of passion, but the *individuals* concerned are not motivated by any such political considerations. Machiavelli saw in the Church an instrument for maintaining civil peace, while his contemporary, St. Catherine of Genoa, found in it the motive and meaning for a life of exceptional charity and devotion. There is a world of difference between the ruler's view and the participant's view.

Up to now the social scientist has looked so closely at the prescribed codes of institutional religion and at their consequences in terms of social control, that he has failed to think of the participant. The person who conforms to a religious custom does so for his own private reasons and derives from his conformity some special significance for his own life. In the Middle East on Fridays one may enter a mosque and witness a sea of humanity kneeling and bending low in the direction of Mecca. The wave of conformity is like that of a vast impersonal tide. Yet, from the point of view of subjective religion, the significance of the devotion is different for each Moslem. All over the world on Sundays millions of

Christians recite a common creed, with innumerable shades of interpretation. Such variety neither invalidates nor weakens any historic faith. It does, however, if properly taken into account, rectify and enrich the approach of both social scientists and theologians to their respective tasks.

Conclusion

The conclusion we come to is that the subjective religious attitude of every individual is, in both its essential and nonessential features, unlike that of any other individual. The roots of religion are so numerous, the weight of their influence in individual lives so varied, and the forms of rational interpretation so endless, that uniformity of product is impossible. Only in respect to certain basic biological functions do men closely resemble one another. In the higher reaches of personality uniqueness of organization becomes more apparent. And since no department of personality is subject to more complex development than the religious sentiment, it is precisely in this area that we must expect to find the ultimate divergences.

This conclusion, I know, will be uncongenial to many. It will offend some scientists who will ask, "How can we possibly classify phenomena that are unique, and does not all science of necessity proceed by classification?" It will disturb some historians and sociologists who like to think that the individual cannot help but mirror the cultural model offered to him as a guide to his development. It will be unpalatable likewise to those theologians and churchmen who deceive themselves by thinking their followers are safely and entirely within some particular ecclesiastical fold.

Yet this conclusion, rightly understood and carefully pondered, will, I maintain, ultimately benefit psychological and social science, and theology as well, if these disciplines will but flex themselves to accommodate the one disturbing truth that there are as many varieties of religious experience as there are religiously inclined mortals upon the earth.

TWO

The Religion of Youth

JUDGED BY ADULT STANDARDS the young child's world of experience is peculiar. Parents are likely to be alternately amused and harassed by their offspring's unruly view of reality. It is not that the child's sensations, pains, and pleasures are so different from the adult's—though from what we know they seem to be comparatively more acute—but the interpretations he places upon them are wholly his own. What to his elders is a stick of kindling wood is to him a beloved doll. What to his elders is a mysterious occurrence, may by him be taken for granted; and what is taken for granted by his elders, may to him be mysterious. Since religion, whatever else it may be, involves meaning and interpretation at every step, we must concede at the outset that religion of childhood is of a very special order, having little in common with the religion of adulthood.

Early Childhood

In infancy, of course, religion is lacking. Desires there are, and a rudimentary social responsiveness; but neither intelligence nor self-consciousness are sufficiently developed to sustain anything that might be called a sentiment, least of all such a highly complex mental organization as the religious sentiment. For this reason the first apparently religious responses of the child are not religious at all, but wholly social in character. They consist at first of trifling habits such as bowing the head or folding the hands, and soon after of learning to repeat simple prayers or hymns. To the child these acts are as routine as brushing the teeth or shaking hands, or any other of the pointless habits required of him by his well-meaning but trying parents. The rituals are learned but not their significance. One child of four had been accustomed to say his nightly prayers before a religious picture. One day he went visiting, and when at night he was bidden to say his prayers he found no picture available. Going to the table he provided himself with the cover of the *Saturday Evening Post* before which, with complete satisfaction, he performed his devotions. And the words of the prayer he said had essentially no different significance for him than the words of his nursery rhymes.

The child's ideas take the best form they can in view of his frail capacity and the scant store of experience at his command. Inevitably his ideas are marked by the egocentricism normal at this stage of life. It could not be otherwise, for every perception and every feeling revolve around the child's growing sense of selfhood. At first he cannot separate thought and feeling from the reality of the external world. By thinking things he makes them happen. Conjuring up the image of a bear, he grows terrified at its menacing appearance. Furthermore, whatever happens is taken to have special reference to himself. Piaget tells how the young child sometimes believes that the sun exists for no other reason than to follow him wherever he goes, in order to see whether he is naughty or good. Many children think a thunderstorm is put on for their own special punishment, just as they think that Santa Claus, whom they often equate with God, pays primary attention to their own private interests. Tommy, at the age of five, entered a church with his mother and noticed the cross upon the altar. "What's that?" he inquired. "A cross," whispered his mother. "Red Cross?" he asked. "No, just a cross." "Oh, I know," said the boy, "T for Tommy." It will be many years before Tommy will be capable of understanding the reverse interpretation of the symbol—that it represents "the I, crossed out."

Kupky tells of an interesting instance of egocentric rationalization in connection with a youthful religious conflict. A boy, reared under stern theology, felt that it was sinful for him to push his wheelbarrow boisterously around the yard, a pastime that he loved above all others. To escape his feelings of guilt he imagined the child Jesus to be, like himself, six years old, and placing Him considerately in the barrow romped with Him endlessly in mutual delight.[1]

Another manifestation of egocentricism lies in the child's insistence that his every "Why?" be answered. If the adult cannot or will not oblige, he calls upon his own inventions, for he is incapable of admitting that in certain matters "one cannot know." The result is that in the child's religion grotesque fantasies abound. Piaget points out that even when the adult supplies an answer it is frequently only partially heard and inaccurately comprehended. Difficult words in the reply slip by and the child takes only the familiar words which he then weaves into a meaning of his own.[2] One lad, hearing that God was high and bright, assumed that the weathercock on the barn must be God, for it was the highest and brightest object he knew. Another, hearing that God was sometimes angry, decided that the stars were caused by the deity who

[1] O. Kupky. *The Religious Development of Adolescents*, New York: Macmillan Co., transl. by W. C. Trow, 1928, p. 29.
[2] J. Piaget. *The Language and Thought of the Child*, New York: Harcourt Brace and Co., transl. 1932, p. 152.

in his moments of wrath punched his cane through the sky thus letting the light of heaven seep through.

Since he can imagine strength far beyond the limits of his own puny abilities, the child almost inevitably develops ideas of power and energy in connection with the deity. His parents are powerful, but God is more so, outdoing even Superman, who in this age of comics, is an unsuspected factor in many children's religious training. Youngsters sometimes evolve their religious concepts in connection with electric storms, a time when fear and helplessness are combined with a sensory manifestation of power.

A further characteristic of the child's early religious concepts is his *anthropomorphism*. How could it be otherwise, since within his world of experience powerful and loving agents are people? Furthermore, he is usually taught that God is, in fact, a male personage. With few exceptions, therefore, children visualize God as an old man, or as a rich man, superman, or king.[3] And, frequently, though not as universally as Freud makes out, God possesses the attributes of the physical father.

Even while the child's mind is spinning in a welter of egocentricism, magical thought, and anthropomorphism, it is being exposed to contrary pressures from the adult environment. The standardized theology and morality of his culture slowly seep through and gradually replace some of the self-centered thinking. A six-year-old boy exemplifies this transitional process. Under manifest personal strain he suddenly refused to say "Our Father." The reason he gave was that God, presumably good, could not be like his earthly father, a drunkard and renegade. The lad had not yet shifted from the concrete imagery of early childhood to the more abstract conception appropriate to later life.

[3] Cf. Kupky. *Op. cit.*, pp. 30–33.

Social learning is a very subtle process. What is taught turns out in the long run to be less important than the manner of teaching. Quite apart from the content of his lessons, the child gains an indelible impression of the sincerity of his parents. Their tone of voice, their example in daily living, are not lost upon the child, even though it may be years before he fully recognizes and appreciates their deeplying piety. Insincerity is perceived as easily as is sincerity, though again it may not be known for what it is until years have elapsed. There is considerable evidence to show that the most religious-minded adults were raised by parents who themselves were deeply religious. It is not that children of pious parents always accept the doctrinal position in which they were trained. Very often they rebel against parental orthodoxy, and yet the sincerity of their parents' outlook has profoundly influenced them. When their own worldly supports break down, they are more likely than not to find their parents' philosophy of life a desirable, though not necessarily a detailed, model to follow.

In the years preceding puberty additional influences are brought to bear on the developing sentiment. For one thing, the child usually encounters grave disappointments and deprivation, and he finds his self-centered prayers, however intense, unavailing. His sick puppy is not spared; the new sled does not come for Christmas. To take this hurdle, and to revise one's views of Providence, passing from self-interest to self-interestedness, is extremely difficult. Many individuals, finding religion no magical aid in this early period, once and for all drop it. An offsetting influence upon development comes from the maturing intelligence which now is able to comprehend somewhat more adequately the abstractions taught at home and in church. The child's theology gradually begins to approximate that of his elders. And normally there is in the pre-puberty period an intense desire to identify with the in-group. Religious practices, if such occur in the family, are taken for granted; and the institutional membership of the parents is rarely questioned. The child asks, "What are we?" and learning that "we" are Presbyterians, requires no further authority for the superiority of Presbyterianism. He fights, if necessary, in its defense, and may go so far as to tear Catholic hair out of Catholic heads, unless given concurrent training in tolerance.

Adolescence

Usually it is not until the stress of puberty that serious reverses occur in the evolution of the religious sentiment. At this period of development the youth is compelled to transform his religious attitudes—indeed all his attitudes—from second-hand fittings to first-hand fittings of his personality. He can no longer let his parents do his thinking for him. Although in some cases the transition is fluent and imperceptible, more often there is a period of rebellion.

Various studies show that for approximately two-thirds of all children there is a reaction against parental and cultural teaching.[4] Approximately half the rebellions come before the age of sixteen and half later. In general the time of insurrection is appreciably earlier for girls than for boys. It takes many forms. Sometimes the youth simply shifts his allegiance to a religious institution different from his parents'. Or he may reach a satisfying rationalism from which religious considerations are forever after eliminated. Sometimes, when the first shadows of doubt appear, he gives up the whole problem and drifts into the style of life, said to be character-

---

[4] Cf. E. D. Starbuck. *Psychology of Religion*, London: W. Scott Co., 1899, p. 232; also G. W. Allport, J. M. Gillespie, J. Young. The religion of the post-war college student, *Journal of Psychology*, 1948, 25, 3–33.

istic of modern youth, of opportunism and hedonism. Occasionally the storm arises not because of intellectual doubts, but because of a gnawing sense of guilt and shame, due perhaps to sex conflicts. Infrequent in the present day are the crises precipitated within evangelical sects which insist upon the necessity for conversion, for a "day of decision."

No subject within the psychology of religion has been more extensively studied than conversion. Various facts are fairly well established. One is that the average age for conversion, like that for the rejection of parental systems of belief, is sixteen, although there is evidence that in recent years the trend is toward an earlier age.[5] One suspects that the impact of movies and radio has sharpened the emotional susceptibilities of children, so that the blandishments of evangelists, if responded to at all, are effective at an earlier age than formerly. We also know that the frequency of conversion experiences varies with cultural conditions. Children in rural areas and in families holding a stern theology are more susceptible than are city children, especially those associated with churches that practice confirmation. Finally, the frequency of abrupt conversions is certainly less today than it was fifty years ago.[6] In the time of our grandparents it was not uncommon for whole families to attend revival campmeetings and to return home with the adolescents formally converted.

Three forms of religious awakening are commonly distinguished, the first being the *definite crisis*, or conversion experience. Of a large group of contemporary college students who reported some form of religious awakening, 14 per cent acknowledged conversion experiences. Fifteen per cent

---

[5] S. L. Pressey, J. E. Janney, R. G. Kuhlen. *Life: A Psychological Survey*, New York: Harper & Bros., 1939, p. 422.

[6] E. T. Clark. *The Psychology of Religious Awakening*, New York: Macmillan, 1929, pp. 50, 87.

reported the second, or *emotional stimulus*, type of awakening, wherein the upheaval is slight or absent, but wherein, nonetheless, the subject is able to designate some single event which served as the effective stimulus to his religious reorientation. Taking these two types together, we have 29 per cent who report that some traumatic or semi-traumatic event underlay their religious development. The remainder of our cases, 71 per cent, report a gradual awakening, with no specifiable occasion being decisive.

Where there has been some marked turn or vivid experience we usually discover consequences of a lasting, and often permanent order. This is not to say that backslidings fail to occur; on the contrary backslidings normally follow any strenuous moral experience. The veil is drawn again after all moments of rapture.[7] But the significance of the definite crisis or emotional stimulus lies in the hunger it arouses, and in the charting of a direction of search for appeasing this hunger. Almost always the individual who has once experienced a vividly religious state of mind seeks throughout his life to recapture its inspiration.

The self-told stories of adolescent religious experience are extraordinarily diverse. Some youths find that religious conviction flares into being overnight; they are amazed to discover that it has taken so violent a hold upon them. Some report the solemn impression made by confirmation or by first communion. Many linger on the dark side of things, and report that for them the religious sentiment is always pensive. Many, perhaps most, experience wavering faith, with peaks of exaltation and troughs of despair. The feeling of alienation from parent and church is common. Moral judgments are often harsh and positive, whether directed toward others or toward oneself. The adolescent is often a moral absolutist and believes that a God must exist in order to guarantee the

---

[7] Cf. W. James. *Op. cit.*, pp. 252 f.

moral values to which he holds. Bereavements and suffering call attention to evil and injustice, and often kindle flames of consuming doubt, or else increase the religious urge, and hasten the development of a religious solution to the problem of evil.

As it grows, the religious sentiment overlaps and blends with other sentiments. The youth who falls in love finds that the exalted selflessness of this state is not unlike the mystical experience he may have in his religious moments. Romantic ideals of accomplishment may occupy his mind, and his ambition may merge with a religious longing to embrace the whole universe. Intense feelings always overflow the boundaries of single sentiments and saturate the personality in all its regions. Art may become an adolescent passion, and youth often finds that religion is only art transposed to a higher key, for like art it seeks to unify and harmonize that with which it deals. But while art unifies within tiny frames of space, religion works within the proscenium of the firmament. Kupky's study of the experience of reverence among adolescents showed that it is most frequently evoked by the stirring beauties of nature.[8] For many adults, as well as adolescents, the aesthetic sense and the religious sense are continuous.

In the American Protestant culture perhaps the most significant influence upon religious development is the fact that youth is normally encouraged to question authority. He is expected, if not by his family, at least by his college and by his contemporaries, to scrutinize critically all established ways of looking at things. He is not only permitted but actively encouraged to find flaws in the school, in the home, in the social system, in the church.[9] For fully two centuries the

[8] *Op. cit.*, p. 102.
[9] One study shows that such questionings are normally associated with considerable conflict if a youth has been reared in the Roman Catholic faith. Cf. C. W. Heath, *et al. What People Are*, Cambridge: Harvard University Press, 1945.

church has been the favorite target of criticism. At its expense wit and reason have been sharpened. Against the convenient ground of orthodoxy countless scientists, philosophers, humanists have displayed to advantage their own brilliant wares. The fashion of the times therefore encourages youth to join the attackers rather than the defenders. Finally, to reject the church of the parent is one way of stepping forth as an independent adult in a culture where the child is expected to outstrip his parents in occupational, social, and educational accomplishments.

College Students

We are now in a position to understand a few facts and figures obtained from a sample of the present generation of college students. The population studied consists of 414 Harvard undergraduates, over two-thirds of them veterans of World War II, and 86 Radcliffe undergraduates. Our results may not be typical for all American youth, certainly not for the youth of other nations. The sample, however, is representative for the two colleges in question, and probably not seriously out of line with the large population of ambitious and intelligent young men and young women now crowding our institutions of higher learning.[10] The material

[10] Recent unpublished replications of our work suggest that our findings do in fact hold surprisingly well for several diverse college populations.

The subjects constituted a virtually complete sample of students enrolled at Harvard and Radcliffe in a course on the "Social and Psychological Foundations of Behavior," during the fall term, 1946–47. The questionnaire was introduced as a part of the program of experiments and demonstrations in the course, and was filled out by the students at their leisure. Nearly every copy was returned. A separate publication presents the questionnaire in full, together with the detailed results which are merely summarized in this chapter; cf. G. W. Allport, J. M. Gillespie, J. Young. *Op. cit.*

was gathered by means of a questionnaire—the traditional but far from perfect method employed in the study of religious sentiments.

The pivotal question in this study reads as follows: "Do you feel that you require some form of religious orientation or belief in order to achieve a fully mature philosophy of life?" This question does not define "religious orientation," but leaves the student free to say whether or not such an orientation, in any sense at all, has a reasonable and necessary place in the economy of his life. To this question seven out of every ten students give an affirmative reply. It would be definitely incorrect to assume that seven in ten are theists, or church-goers, or traditionalists. We can say only that, given an opportunity to define religion in any way at all, seven out of ten students regard themselves as actually or potentially religious.

Looking first at the individuals giving a negative reply, that is, those who do not feel the need of some religious orientation in their lives, what do we discover? For one thing, males are more often in this category than females. Whereas 82 per cent of the women students report need for a religious orientation, the corresponding figure among non-veteran men is 76 per cent, and among veterans 64 per cent. It is common in all studies to find women more interested in religion however defined. They are more often the church-goers, more often devout in their personal lives, and more often the family mentors in matters of religion. But it is well to guard against exaggerating this finding, for the measured differences between the sexes seldom exceed 20 per cent.

Besides sex difference and war experience (which I shall later discuss), the age factor turns out to be important. Young men of twenty or under more often feel the need of a religious orientation than do their fellow students who are twenty-one or over. There is good reason to suppose that on the average the early and middle twenties are, in fact, the least religious period of life. It is then that the alienation from the parental codes has become complete. It is then also that youth feels most secure in pursuing his life ambition. He has not yet had the rude shock that comes to nearly all adults when they first realize that their abilities and probable accomplishments are, after all, not likely to equal their aims and pretensions. In the early twenties the youth, as a rule, has not yet married a wife who, by the law of averages, will be more religious than he is. Nor has he yet undertaken the training of children. When he does so he will probably want them to have the benefit of religious influence which is part of the cultural heritage. Nor, in the early and middle twenties has he yet developed sufficient perspective upon his own upbringing to appreciate the sincerity and piety that may have marked his parents' attitudes. It is often in the thirties that people first decide the parental model is, after all, not a bad one to follow. The old folks now seem to have been acting as wisely as they could have done in the face of life's mysteries and difficulties.

Let us look next at the influences of childhood upbringing upon those who deny the need for a religious orientation in their lives. First we note that religious influence upon children is by no means a thing of the past as it is often thought to be. In 19 per cent of our cases religion is reported to have been a "very marked" influence in upbringing, in 42 per cent a "moderate" influence, in 33 per cent "slight," and in less than 7 per cent non-existent. Now students who report religion to have been a marked or even a moderate influence are much more likely to express the need for a religious orientation. If the influence is reported to have been slight or non-existent, the need is less often felt. But there are striking exceptions: some who report "marked influence" are sharp in their reaction against it. And, on the other hand, a third of those who had "no influence at all" yet develop a sense of present need. It is well to be clear about the role of upbringing. No single psychological or environmental factor is as important in creating a need for religion as is early training, and yet this factor is not decisive. As I have just said, a third of our students who report no influence in their upbringing at all, yet somehow have developed a religious proclivity.

Turning to the *kind* of religious upbringing that surrounded our students we discover additional facts of interest. Among those who were reared in the Roman Catholic faith (15 per cent of our total sample) nearly all now report a need for some religious orientation in their lives. At the other extreme are those who were brought up in some form of Judaism or in liberalized Protestantism (defined in our questionnaire as including Unitarianism and Universalism). Fully 40 per cent of the youth raised under either of these forms of faith fail to regard the religious sentiment as a necessary component in their personalities. We note, however, that these two faiths, as contrasted with the Roman Catholic, were, by and large, regarded as "slight" rather than as "marked" influences, and so we are unable to determine whether it may not, after all, be the *degree* of influence rather than the *kind* that is decisive. Were Unitarians, let us say, required to attend church every Sunday, and to participate as actively in religious practices, their children might develop a religious hunger as frequently as do the Catholic children.

One final fact concerning the third of our cases who do not feel the need for religious orientation in their lives: they did not, by any means, all give an unequivocally negative answer to our question. About 38 per cent of them said they were "doubtful" about the whole matter. Hence, out of the total student sample, actually only 18 per cent replied positively that for them maturity of personality requires no religion. We are led back then to our primary conclusion, namely that in the large majority of these students' lives, even in this age of technology and social disintegration when skepticism hangs heavy upon the horizon—even today the disposition of youth to seek *some* kind of religion is apparent.

Among those who allow the religious sentiment a place in their lives, what influences do they themselves feel to underlie their sense of need? Taking the factors they mention in order of frequency, we find *parents* designated in 67 per cent of the cases, and *other human beings* in 57 per cent. Thus the factor of personal influences looms largest. Next comes *fear*, mentioned by 51 per cent of these students. The *church* is recognized as a specific influence by 40 per cent, and *gratitude* (an emotion generally neglected in our social life) by 37 per cent. There follow *aesthetic appeals* and *reading*, in about a third of the cases. Then comes the pressure of sheer *conformity* with tradition, acknowledged by 27 per cent. Studies influenced one-quarter, and *sorrow* or *bereavement* 18 per cent of the cases. A *mystical experience*, something not fully understood, was reported by 17 per cent, and the ravages of *sex turmoil* by 16 per cent. The lesson we learn from this survey is that the psychological roots of the religious sentiment—even those that can be consciously reported—are very numerous, and that for one who is religiously inclined almost any type of experience can be, and will be, redacted into the channel of the growing sentiment.

Next we inquire how the religious views of these students compare with their parents' views. The question was asked, "How in general does the firmness of your belief in religion compare with your mother's belief?" Only 8 per cent thought their beliefs were more firm than their mothers', whereas half thought they were less firm. The remainder felt they were about the same, or else did not know. In all probability three causes contribute to this result. There is, first of all, the sex difference. The majority of our cases are male, and religious interests, as we know, are on the average less strongly developed in men than in women. There is likewise the age difference. With passing years the intensity of the religious sentiment in the son or daughter will in some cases equal or surpass the mother's. Finally, there is undoubtedly a residual influence of genuine secularization. The present generation probably does manifest less firmness of structure in the religious sentiment than did the parental generation. The students also reported that their beliefs are, on the whole, less firm than their fathers' beliefs. Here the interesting facts emerge that fathers are regarded as considerably less religious than mothers, and that twice as many students profess to be ignorant of the strength of their fathers' faith as of their mothers'. It seems that sons and daughters find it relatively more difficult, in religious matters, to learn where their fathers stand.

Now we come to a most striking finding in our comparison of generations. The students who expressed a need for some religious orientation were asked whether on the whole the tradition of one of the following great religious systems seemed satisfactorily to meet their need: Roman Catholicism, Anglo-Catholicism or Eastern Orthodoxy, Protestant Christianity, liberalized Christianity (defined as including Unitarianism, Universalism), an ethical but not a theological Christianity (defined as including humanism, ethical culture), some form of Judaism, or some other which they were allowed to specify. As a further alternative they were permitted to say that "a substantially new type of religion is required." They were also asked to indicate the character of the religious influence that prevailed in their own upbringing, the same system of classification being used. From the responses thus obtained it is possible to characterize the shifts in allegiance that have occurred. It turns out that only about 60 per cent of the students who feel the need for a religious orientation find the system in which they were reared satisfactory to their needs. It is fair to report, however, that among the Roman Catholic students who still feel the need for religion 85 per cent express themselves as satisfied with this system of faith.

To illustrate the reshuffling that has taken place in this generation, let us look at the 200 instances of students who report that they were brought up in the more orthodox Protestant churches. Exactly one-quarter of these cases have turned irreligious, declaring that for a mature personality they need no religious orientation of any kind whatsoever. Fourteen per cent of them claim that a new type of religion is needed altogether. An additional 19 per cent shift their allegiance to more liberal forms of Christianity—to Unitarianism perhaps, or to an ethical but entirely nontheological Christianity. We are left with precisely 85 cases, or 42 per cent, who are content to stay within the tradition in which they were reared. The defection is equally great for Judaism and for all other systems of Christian beliefs represented, with the sole exception of Roman Catholicism. The drift throughout seems to be from theocentric emphasis toward ethical emphasis.

Among these youths orthodox faith in theological dogma is waning fast, faster than are religious practices. Certain questions were asked dealing with church attendance, prayer, and subjective feelings of reverence and dependence on a Supreme Being. From the answers we learn that only 15 per cent of the students deny altogether engaging in any religious practices or experiencing any religious states of mind during the preceding six months' period. This finding must mean that many of the students who report that they need no religion in their lives yet engage in some occasional religious practice. We learn that 35 per cent of all women students and 15 per cent of men say their prayers every day;

while an additional 40 per cent of the women, and 50 per cent of the men, pray occasionally though not every day. Only 38 per cent of the women and 17 per cent of the men attend church every week, but the majority do so occasionally. Four-fifths of the women and three-fifths of the men report at least occasional experiences of reverence, devotion, or dependence on a Supreme Being. Religious inclination, and even traditional religious practice, are considerably more prominent than is orthodoxy of belief.

If we were to estimate the extent of belief in the historic pattern of orthodox Christian doctrine, we should arrive at a figure in the neighborhood of 25 per cent. This estimate of the extent of orthodoxy can be made with the aid of various questions. One, for example, deals with Christology. Only 28 per cent of the students subscribe to the view that "Christ, as the Gospels state, should be regarded as divine— as the human incarnation of God." Well over half prefer the view that "Christ should be regarded merely as a great prophet or teacher, much as the Mohammedans accept Mahomet, or as the Chinese accept Confucius." As regards immortality only one-quarter of the students subscribe to the belief in "personal immortality, i.e., the continued exist- ence of the soul as an individual and separate entity." Sim- ilarly, a rigidly defined theistic view of the deity attracts the support of only one-fifth of the men and two-fifths of the women. This view is stated in the questionnaire as belief in "an infinitely wise, omnipotent Creator of the universe and of natural laws, whose protection and favor may be suppli- cated through worship and prayer. God is a personal God." It is not true, however, that the majority of students are atheists. On the contrary, only about 12 per cent consider themselves atheists and an additional 20 per cent agnostics, saying that "because of our necessary ignorance in this matter, I neither believe nor disbelieve in God." The remainder of the students prefer to express their views in broadly deistic or pantheistic terms.

In this connection we report that there is little support for the Marxist position that religion is the opiate of the people, and that active resistance to organized religious forces is needed in order that people may rightfully claim what is theirs without the reactionary handicap of religious faith. Twelve per cent agree with this extreme position and an additional 12 per cent express no opinion. Seventy-six per cent disagree sharply with it.

Even though the majority have a belief in a God of some kind, the majority likewise, with seeming inconsistency, subscribe to the essentially humanistic proposition, as expressed by John Dewey, "If religion is to play a useful role in life, it should be regarded entirely as a natural human function; it should have nothing whatever to do with supernatural notions." Perhaps the unfortunate word "notion" in this statement biases the answers, for who wishes his religion to deal with mere notions—supernatural or otherwise? And yet to some extent the inconsistency undoubtedly reflects a confusion on the part of many students, who by their own account need religion, and have some type of belief in God, and yet who, at the same time, attempt to rule out the supernatural from their idea of what religion should be.

To interpret this inconsistency I think we need to regard the rejection of supernaturalism as an additional expression of dissatisfaction with the churches whose specific brand of supernaturalism as the students conceive it is unpopular. Discontent with the traditional ecclesiastical positions—especially the Protestant and Jewish—is shown by much of the evidence already cited. In addition we find a high degree of agreement with the proposition that "denominational distinctions, at least within Protestant Christianity, are out of date, and may as well be eliminated as rapidly as possible." Fifty-seven per cent of all students agree with the ecumenicists in this matter; only 19 per cent disagree, and the remainder have no opinion. Differences of temperament, no doubt, will always require varying styles of worship; and the theological disputes which originally underlay denominational distinctions are regarded by a clear majority of our students as an anachronism.

May we sum up by saying that (1) most students feel the need of including a religious sentiment somewhere within their maturing personalities; (2) for the most part they believe in a God, though their view is not usually of the traditional theistic variety; (3) a bare quarter are in essential matters orthodox and historically faithful to theological dogma; (4) the majority maintain some of the forms of traditional religious practices including prayer; (5) but the majority are clearly dissatisfied with institutional religion as it exists, so much so that 40 per cent of those who feel a religious need yet repudiate the church in which they were reared. If we take the entire student population who have had a religious upbringing, including those who feel no religious need and those who do, we find that 56 per cent reject the church in which they were trained.

It would be wrong to imply that these findings are peculiar to the present college generation. We know that for years the trends here described have been under way. A study conducted at the University of Syracuse in 1926, for example, revealed that half the students at that time felt that, while they needed religion in their own lives, the current practices of the church were unsatisfactory. Only about one-third felt that on the whole these practices were satisfactory —an estimate much like that obtained in the present study. Further, in respect to attitudes toward the diety, actually fewer of the Syracuse students in 1926 endorsed the extreme theistic position, although at the same time a smaller percentage endorsed agnosticism or atheism. Whereas at Syracuse only about 10 per cent abstained altogether from church attendance and devotional practices, our figure is nearer to one-third. We must, of course, remember that not only a difference of time is here involved but also a different type of college population.[11]

One additional comparison in time is of interest. A certain question included in our survey was identical with a question asked of 3,000 students at the University of Wisconsin in 1930. It had to do with attitudes toward the church. Very few in either institution subscribed to the position that the "Church is one sure and infallible foundation of civilized life"—6 per cent at Cambridge and 4 per cent at Wisconsin. But the second most favorable answer showed a significant difference. "On the whole," the statement reads, "the Church stands for the best in human life, although certain minor shortcomings and errors are necessarily apparent in it, as in all human institutions." To this proposition 37 per cent of Harvard and Radcliffe students in 1946 give assent, but only 24 per cent of Wisconsin students of both sexes in 1930. Correspondingly, statements markedly unfavorable to the church received much more endorsement sixteen years ago than today.[12]

Such trend studies as are available, therefore, show that the disaffection of modern youth is probably no greater today than it was fifteen or twenty years ago. The problem is perennial, probably has been so for the last hundred years, perhaps longer.

If youthful disaffection is so great how does it happen that institutional religion continues? Surely if half the student population in each generation desert the church of their an-

---

[11] D. Katz and F. H. Allport. *Students' Attitudes*, Syracuse: Craftsman Press, 1931, pp. 261, 280, 290.

[12] Cf. W. H. Sheldon. *The Varieties of Human Temperament*, New York: Harper & Bros., 1942, pp. 496–498.

cestors, with few new student adherents being won, it ought not to take long for a vanishing point to be reached. The answer to this puzzle lies in two considerations. After the irreligious twenties, the period with which we are here dealing, many young people do in fact return willingly, and sometimes enthusiastically, to the institutional forms from which they rebelled. Secondly, as we have seen, the vestiges of loyalty as reflected in nominal membership and at least occasional church attendance, linger on even among youth who have virtually lost their allegiance to church doctrine. So, on the whole, the church as an institution is less affected than is the dogmatic faith of its youthful members. By enlarging its social activities and by intensifying good works the Protestant church at least is able to preserve a certain vitality, but with a shifting function.

There remains one aspect of the loss of theocentric faith and the drift to non-theological liberalism to be considered. The shift is unquestionably due in part, though not entirely, to the ignorance of students today regarding the teachings of theology. The "queen of the sciences" has fallen from her throne. Were evidence needed we could point to the decline of doctrinal and Biblical teaching in church schools, to the lack of college courses dealing with the tenets of faith, to the reports of many chaplains in the armed services who found only the densest of ignorance of historic doctrine. One may read student autobiographies dealing with personal religious history without finding the slightest comprehension of the theological position which they, more likely than not, are in the process of rejecting. Even more certainly are students ignorant of the reasoned doctrines of Hinduism, Mohammedanism, and all the other great faiths. Lacking a knowledge of comparative religion and of theology, young people cannot have available the solutions reached by great minds in the past even when they are ripe to use them. They

know next to nothing of St. Thomas Aquinas, Meister Eck-
hardt, Luther, Calvin, Wesley, Swedenborg, Kierkegaard,
Newman, Tyrrell, Ritschl, Barth, Bowne, Niebuhr, or any
other of the brilliant minds who have wrestled with the
rational aspects of the Christian faith. These thinkers are
no less aware than the critical undergraduate of today of the
intellectual difficulties involved, and of the degree to which
institutional religion falls short of its professions. The positions they have achieved are hard won, and possibly valid
for themselves alone. But their efforts, nonetheless, might
serve as models of the strenuous thinking demanded of every
aspirant seeking religious maturity.

Veterans

Before leaving the period of late youth we examine our
data to determine the effects of the recent war upon the religious attitudes of veterans. In studying the 290 sincere and
candid reports written by veterans one is struck by certain
uniformities, but even more by the underlying diversities.
To consider first the impression of diversity, I submit three
contrasting statements, all written by men with combat experience, all of Protestant background. One veteran wrote:

War is the final proof: (1) that there is no God; (2) that
religion is a failure. How can you believe in a beneficient
deity when millions of innocent people are dying needlessly?
If religion were effective, there could be no war, hatred,
persecution, bigotry, starvation, selfishness, imperialism, and
colonial exploitation.
Religion has tried for centuries to establish a brotherhood
of man. It has had its day. The people should wake up and
realize how futile it is, and what hypocrites they are.
The problems religion tries to solve need solving, but religion has failed. I am interested in seeing them solved, but
must look to other institutions.

Another veteran of my acquaintance had been unusually devout. While lying in no man's land waiting to attack he was praying. At that very moment a bomb burst close by. He lost one arm, was disfigured and blinded. At that instant, he reports, he became a total and militant atheist. Yet, another blinded veteran reports that for his handicap he has received abundant compensation in the inner light and peace that has come to him along with an awakened faith.

As an instance of a quietly sustained private faith we have this statement:

If I had not had a personal religious philosophy when I entered combat I do not believe that I would have lasted at all. For me it was most definitely a source of strength. I require no one else to hold my beliefs but I experience intense personal comfort from them myself. I can think of no other single thing that sustains me day by day so much as my personal belief in God. I can't hold it out to other people because I really can't explain it.

And between the antis and the pros there are many confessions of perplexity and groping. A typical instance is this:

I find myself highly confused. Don't believe in any organized religion, but do believe in the innate goodness of man. I believe in the Christian virtues, but not in the Christian religion.
I was struck by how untouched the majority appeared to be by the basic and simplest principles of religion with respect to charity to one's neighbor, etc. I was convinced therefore that the only possible way to change or to improve this situation is to substitute some system of reasonable ethics for present denominational beliefs.

This statement is representative of the situation that so commonly exists in many minds today—Christian ethics outlasting Christian doctrine.

The diversity of these statements speaks for itself. As so often happens in the development of personality, the crises of existence tend merely to intensify the style of life which was in any case developing. Occasionally, of course, there are abrupt changes, but usually these turn out on closer scrutiny to be accentuations of what was previously a latent tendency.

From the statistical point of view we find that 55 per cent of the veterans say that the war made them neither more nor less religious than they were before. Twenty-six per cent, however, claim that it made them *more* religious, and only 19 per cent that it made them *less* so. This is an interesting result in view of the fact that on most of the other questions, especially those dealing with conventional religious beliefs and practices, veterans turn out to be more dissident than non-veterans. Likewise we recall that among veterans a slightly larger percentage said that they needed no religious orientation in their personalities. These apparent inconsistencies may be reconciled in a single conclusion: the war created a few more anti-religious attitudes than are present among non-veterans, but in those retaining a religious sentiment the effect was to intensify its prominence.

It still remains true that nearly two-thirds of the veterans reported a need for a religion in their lives. To the question whether war experience made them more or less *interested* in the problems religion seeks to answer, 58 per cent replied, "more." Only 5 per cent said they became less interested. Here perhaps is the clearest indication of all that the war experience was one of critical intensity, and created in contemporary youth a level of interest probably not equaled in any previous generation during the modern age. But the increased interest has not been accompanied by a proportionately augmented faith.

Among the veterans who had decided that their personalities required no religious faith, and among those who were doubtful about the matter—36 per cent in all—the development of a humanitarian substitute can often be detected. In a functional sense these veterans have replaced a religious faith with ethical meliorism. For example, in the following statement there is an integrating zeal devoid of the metaphysical wish.

Why will individuals be so foolish and hypocritical as to spend time and money on religion when intensive programs conducted against TB, venereal disease, cancer, polio, etc. with the same energy and money, would wipe out these dread diseases? . . . Organized religion will always be prey to graft and hypocrisy and can never be just. It is merely another schism in a divided world—a curse.

This tirade is somewhat exceptional. In most cases, among disbelievers as well as believers, there is evidence of sympathy for all forms of religious yearning, and respect for whatever solution an individual in his own conscience has achieved. This tolerance, it should be noted, is directed more toward individuals than toward institutionalized religion or its representatives. Only one veteran had a favorable remark to make regarding the chaplain of his unit. Many more were critical. But perhaps the conditions of the study invited critical rather than appreciative comment.

Complaints regarding the clergy generally have one principal basis—their alleged ineptness in handling human relationships. Though few of the veterans seem to have heard of the current movement to provide clinical training for the clergy, it is certain that they would heartily endorse it. For they seem to feel that chaplains during the war were lacking techniques appropriate to the cure of souls. Even those chaplains whose churches provided them objective, sacramental aids are felt to need additional training in modern psychological and administrative skills.

We turn, in conclusion, to the fighting man in combat, under conditions of great stress. There, by his own report, he stands revealed as a praying animal. Without the evidence of our study, I for one should not have prejudiced how truly universal is the impulse to pray in times of stress. I should have thought that irreligious personalities would have resisted, even in times of extremity, acts entirely foreign to the customary frame of their personalities. And, of course, some of them did behave consistently in this regard. Several veterans denied having even the slightest inclination to pray. But they were the exceptions. Far more characteristic is this report:

Eight months of infantry combat in Europe made me during that period very religious. Some days I prayed continuously. During the Battle of the Bulge all I did was fight, eat, and pray to stay awake, alert, alive.

Especially revealing is the statement which reads:

I flew 30 missions over Germany in a bomber. As the going got rougher I would just hope all the harder that we would get out of harm's way. Fear motivated the hoping, and where hoping ends and prayer begins I don't know.

In this statement lies an important insight. Prayer is continuous with hope, as hope is continuous with fear. Religious activity thus grows imperceptibly out of desire. The mind finds itself gradually stretching beyond the limits of its own adaptive capacity, seeking to add to its natural powers a reasonable complement. In some people, as in this veteran, the sense of complementation occurs only in times of crisis; in others it occurs every day in a variety of ways whenever mundane activities seem suddenly to belong to some eternal scheme.

Many of our reporters expressed the opinion that "everyone prays in one way or another when he is in combat." One, however, varies the point slightly: "There were atheists in foxholes," he writes, "but most of them were in love." Here we have another shrewd insight: the individual in distress craves affection and security. Sometimes a human bond will suffice, more often it will not. Prayer in foxholes is undoubtedly a religious act, but from the point of view of solid development of the religious sentiment, a foxhole is a poor place in which to learn to pray, for the religion of a merely frightened man is likely to evaporate as soon as danger is removed.

Oddly mixed with skepticism and humor is the following philosophy of prayer:

After seeing many of the habitual churchgoers killed, and realizing that they prayed as much, perhaps more than I, I decided that prayer had no survival value for me. To be sure I still prayed, but it seems to me now that it was a case of being on the safe side if I did get killed. I don't believe in a hereafter now that I am leading a less hazardous life, but at the same time it seems like a good idea to keep on the good side of whatever powers there be. There is no point in shoveling coal if one has a chance of playing a harp.

The efficacy of prayer as a means of personal protection worried many. "My closest friend and myself never prayed," writes one veteran, "and were never even wounded. I saw one boy praying and killed during his prayer by a German 88 shell."

Violent and perplexing shocks of this order bring doubts and rejection. Combat veterans have seen human suffering at its most intense. They have beheld the march of the unleashed forces of evil. Before their eyes have unrolled the very facts that are hardest to reconcile with the existence of a God. Further, they have lived at a time and in a situation where there is no longer a prevailing climate of belief. Thus the last traces of their childhood religion have been forcibly wiped out. Should they yet find a way of satisfying the religious need which, in spite of everything, in most of them persists, they will do so only by way of the religion of maturity.

THREE

The Religion of Maturity

A PERSON of twenty, thirty, or even seventy, years of age does not necessarily have an adult personality. In fact, chronological age is a comparatively poor measure of mental and emotional maturity, likewise of religious maturity. In emerging from childhood one gives up the egocentricism of his thought and feeling only under pressure, and ordinarily environmental pressure does not force a maturity of religious outlook upon the individual as inexorably as it does other forms of maturity. For the individual's religion is usually regarded by others as his own business and, so far as others care, can easily remain egocentric, magical, and wish-fulfilling. Hence, in probably no region of personality do we find so many residues of childhood as in the religious attitudes of adults.

Maturity in any sentiment comes about only when a growing intelligence somehow is animated by the desire that this sentiment shall not suffer arrested development, but shall keep pace with the intake of relevant experience. In many people, so far as the religious sentiment is concerned, this inner demand is absent. Finding their childhood religion to have comforting value and lacking outside pressure, they cling to an essentially juvenile formulation. Often they retain it to preserve pleasant associations accumulated in childhood, or because conformity to the *status quo* insures present comfort and social position. They take over the ancestral religion much as they take over the family jewels. It would be awkward to bring it into too close a relationship with science, with suffering, and with criticism.

Nor shall we gauge the maturity of religion by a predetermined standard of belief or practice that we personally are pleased to approve. To say that your views or my views are mature, and to impose them as a test of maturity upon all other views would be impertinent. Discussions of religion are usually marked by the assumption that the beliefs of the writer are superior to all other varieties of belief.

The criteria of maturity should be more objective, drawn from a defensible theory of the nature of human personality. Elsewhere I have argued that the attributes of a mature personality are three in number.[1] First, a variety of psychogenic interests is required which concern themselves with ideal objects and values beyond the range of viscerogenic desire. Unless one escapes the level of immediate biological impulse, one's life is manifestly dwarfed and infantile. A second attribute is the ability to objectify oneself, to be reflective and insightful about one's own life. The individual with insight sees himself as others see him, and at certain moments glimpses himself in a kind of cosmic perspective. A developed sense of humor is an aspect of this second attribute. Finally, a mature personality always has some unifying philosophy of life, although not necessarily religious in type, nor articulated in words, nor entirely complete. But without the direction and coherence supplied by some dominant integrative pattern any life seems fragmented and aimless.

These three attributes of maturity are not selected in an

[1] G. W. Allport. *Personality: A Psychological Interpretation*, New York: Henry Holt & Co., 1937, Chapter 8.

arbitrary manner. They are chosen because they represent the three primary avenues of development that are open to any human being in the course of his growth: the avenue of widening interests (the expanding self), the avenue of detachment and insight (self-objectification), and the avenue of integration (self-unification). I doubt that any scientifically supported criteria of maturity would differ substantially from these three.

Not every mature individual forms a religious sentiment. If he does not, it is because he has some other satisfactory philosophy of life, a mode of synthesis that is perhaps aesthetic, ethical, or philosophical in character. But whenever in a mature personality a mature religious sentiment does develop it has a heavy duty to perform, for it is charged with the task of accommodating every atom of experience that is referred to it. Other master sentiments are ordinarily less ambitious in their scope. A thoroughly aesthetic person, for example, may evolve what for him is an adequate style of life. With art and humor he makes out well enough, but he does so because he declares many of the moral and metaphysical puzzles of life to be of no great consequence to him. By contrast, the mature religious sentiment lays itself open to all facts, to all values, and disvalues, and claims to have the clue to their theoretical and practical inclusion in a frame of life. With such a task to perform it is impossible for this sentiment in a mature stage of development to remain disconnected from the mainstream of experience, relegated to a corner of the fantasy life where it provides an escape clause in one's contract with reality.

Most of the criticism of religion is directed to its immature forms. When immature it has not evolved beyond the level of impulsive self-gratification. Instead of dealing with psychogenic values it serves either a wish-fulfilling or soporific function for the self-centered interests. When immature it does not entail self-objectification, but remains unreflective, failing to provide a context of meaning in which the individual can locate himself, and with perspective judge the quality of his conduct. Finally, the immature sentiment is not really unifying in its effect upon the personality. Excluding, as it does, whole regions of experience, it is spasmodic, segmented, and even when fanatic in intensity, it is but partially integrative of the personality.

The Nature of Sentiment

When I use the term sentiment, I might equally well for our purpose speak of *interest, outlook,* or *system of beliefs.* All these terms simply call attention to the fact that in the course of development relatively stable units of personality gradually emerge. Such units are always the product of the two central and vital functions of mental life: *motivation* and *organization.* Motivation refers to the "go" of mental life, organization to its patterning. It is regrettable, as I have previously said, that our psychological vocabulary inclines us to separate the two—the emotional forces from the cognitive or organizing forces. From the point of view of actual conduct the primary unit of mental life is *organized motive,* or, if you prefer, *motivated organization.* Whatever it is called, this unit is a system of readiness, a mainspring of conduct, preparing the person for adaptive behavior whenever the appropriate stimulus or associations are presented.

If a system of readiness is well ingrained and fairly specific, such as that involved in driving an automobile, we are likely to speak of a *habit.* If it represents a somewhat broader style of adapting without reference to specific stimulus, such as dispositions leading to politeness, aggressiveness, timidity in conduct, we speak of a *trait.* If it represents a tendency dis-

connected from the individual's socialized dispositions and
warring with them, we are likely to speak of a *neurosis*. If it
represents an organization of feeling and thought directed
toward some definable object of value—a mother, a son, a
keepsake, a neighborhood, a fatherland—we call the system
sentiment. The object of a sentiment need not be as physi-
cally concrete as those just named. A sentiment may also
deal with more abstract ideas of value, as in the devotion
some people have to beauty, or to the sacredness of personality, or to the idea One World. Besides such positive
sentiments, there are of course negative sentiments wherein
aversion is felt to persons, objects, ideas that are regarded
by the individual not as values but as disvalues. Thus an
atheist may have a negative sentiment relating to all things
commonly regarded as religious.

At the level of the more abstract sentiments we encounter
difficulty in designating the precise object to which the individual is attached. Can we prescribe, for example, what
the object or focus of the religious sentiment must be? I
think not, for the sentiment is so broad that it constitutes
a mere posture of the mind that persists while various objects
and sub-values are successively brought into view. At one
moment a certain aspect of the deity may engage the individual's attention; soon he finds himself thinking of the
nature of evil, and then of the chances for immortality; a
moment of adoration intervenes; and then another aspect
of the deity is brought to mind, which perhaps fixes attention upon the significance of some sacrament, and this in
turn arouses a special attitude toward some item in the creed.
And so it goes endlessly, ardor rising and falling as different
objects and sub-values of the sentiment are present in the
mind. It is common to find people who are much alike in
some component attitudes and very unlike in others.

The astonishing thing about the religious sentiment, and

to a less degree about any sentiment, is that, although it entails many component attitudes and objects of interest, it represents nonetheless a stable unit of mental life. The component attitudes are variable but all contribute to a single well-patterned system.

Shall we then define the mature religious sentiment as a *disposition, built up through experience, to respond favorably, and in certain habitual ways, to conceptual objects and principles that the individual regards as of ultimate importance in his own life, and as having to do with what he regards as permanent or central in the nature of things*? Thus defined, the religious sentiment allows wide variation both in the human race at large and during the course of any single individual's development.

Unless we are dealing with a religious genius—Christ being the example—we must not expect that the religious sentiment, even when mature, will be absolutely consistent. More than with other sentiments, its fashioning is always unfinished business. Such a heavy assignment, the synthesis of all facts and forces "central in the nature of things," calls for more than can be accomplished. A person with even a strongly developed religious sentiment still finds that his conduct does not issue as uniformly as he wishes from its directive control. Impulse often wins out, and many of the things he would not do he does; and much that he would do he leaves undone. If the religious sentiment were perfectly organized and in sole control there would be no discrepancy between profession and practice. But, excepting in a religious genius, such a degree of integrated direction of conduct is never achieved.

While we guard against overestimating the consistency and completeness of the mature religious sentiment, we may nonetheless list the attributes that mark it off from the immature sentiment. By comparison, the mature sentiment is (1) well differentiated; (2) dynamic in character in spite of its derivative nature; (3) productive of a consistent morality; (4) comprehensive; (5) integral; and (6) fundamentally heuristic. It will be seen that these criteria are nothing else than special applications in the religious sphere of the tests for maturity of personality: a widened range of interests, insight into oneself, and the development of an adequately embracing philosophy of life.

Differentiation of the Mature Sentiment

When we say that mature religious sentiment is differentiated we are calling attention to its richness and complexity. In any single life this sentiment is almost certain to be more complex, more subtle, and more personal in flavor, than any single definition of religion can possibly suggest. According to Westermarck, religion is "a regardful attitude towards a supernatural being, on whom man feels himself dependent and to whom he makes an appeal in his worship." And so it often is. MacMurray introduces a social note, regarding the aim of religion as human perfection in relation with others, as a realization of fellowship. Religion often has this social emphasis. But Whitehead introduces the opposite note, defining religion as "what a man does with his solitariness" and as the "longing of the spirit that the facts of existence should find their justification in the nature of existence."[2] All of these, and many additional points of emphasis are valid; but it is sheer presumption to suppose that one formulation captures the completeness or precise emphasis of the sentiment as it exists in any single mature adult.

The multiplicity of interests that fall within the religious

[2] Collections containing these and additional definitions may be found in H. A. Murray and C. D. Morgan. A clinical study of sentiments, II, Genetic Psychology Monographs, 1945, pp. 32, 153–311; also in Edward Brightman. Philosophy of Religion, New York: Prentice Hall, 1940, pp. 13–18.

sentiment I designate as "differentiations" of this sentiment. It is better to do this than to regard them as myriads of separate sentiments: toward the church, toward the divine, toward world brotherhood, toward good and evil. For it is evident that these components, though discriminable, are woven into a pattern. There are dominant and subsidiary designs in this pattern characteristic of each individual's personal life.

Those who have not developed a differentiated sentiment often show a kind of uncritical abandon. They may say, "I don't know enough about it to be rational; I'm accepting my religion on purely emotional grounds," or, "I believe what I was taught, and that's good enough for me." There is here no reflective articulation of parts.

The distinction between the undifferentiated and the differentiated sentiment is illustrated by two students' descriptions of their fathers. One wrote, "Dad is a perfect father. He loves his family and his family loves him. . . . He is looked up to in all the town, highly admired. . . . He will help anyone. He is noted for his fairness and honesty. Fairness and honesty are Dad." This encomium betrays an undifferentiated sentiment. The father is just perfect, everything about him is right. The student's devotion to him is marked by such abandon that we suspect she has never made a close and analytic inspection of his character, and even that her lavish praise may cover some repressed animosity. Detailed study of this case shows this suspicion to be justified. Deep inside the girl dislikes many things about her father, though she denies this dislike even to herself. The sentiment therefore emerges as an oversimplified disposition, not well integrated with the deeper life of the subject.

Another daughter describes her father in the following way: "He is somewhat unsocial, but dramatic enough to be pleasing in company; irritable, but not at all ill-natured; conscientious, hard-working, puritanical; timid in some things, dogged in others. His imagination is shown in his love of travel, but is not much in evidence otherwise." This daughter likewise approves of her father. Yet, unlike the first, she is observant, critical, not merely abandoned in her admiration. One suspects that the very *differentiation* of the sentiment in the second case prevents repressed criticisms and hostility from forming. Her view of her father, if more complex, is more realistic.[3]

Now evidence shows that the very subjects who accept religion unreflectively and uncritically tend to react in an equally unreflective way to their parents, to political issues, to social institutions. Their sentiments seem uniformly immature. They are found usually to have repressed conflicts. In them, hostility, anxiety, prejudice, are detectable by psychological methods. Recent investigations, for example, have uncovered the fact that among people with strong religious sentiments race prejudice is often marked. Closer analysis indicates that the religious sentiment in these cases is blindly institutional, exclusionist, and related to self-centered values. Among people with reflective and highly differentiated sentiments, race prejudice is rarely found.[4]

A differentiated sentiment is the outgrowth of many successive discriminations and continuous reorganization. Commencing in later childhood or adolescence the individual who is on the way to maturity probably will repudiate both the oversimplified product of his earlier egocentric thinking, and

[3] These cases, together with other evidence bearing upon our conclusions, are contained in a series of three papers by Vera V. French: The structure of sentiments, *Journal of Personality*, 1947, 15, 247–282; 1947, 16, 78–108; 1947, 16, 209–244.

[4] Cf. E. Frenkel-Brunswik and R. N. Sanford. Some personality factors in anti-Semitism, *Journal of Psychology*, 1945, 20, 271–291; also G. W. Allport and B. M. Kramer. Some roots of prejudice, *Journal of Psychology*, 1946, 22, 9–39.

blind conformity to institutional or parental views. He discovers that the literal-minded and second-hand faith that he previously held now needs emendation. He sees the evasions and escapist dangers of his original beliefs. He perceives the shortcomings of tradition even while he appreciates its virtues. Whole sections of humanity, he observes, have halted at the performance of empty ritual or at a belief in the supernatural which squares neither with science nor with experience. The authoritarianism and conceit of entrenched ecclesiasticism may revolt him. Religion, he now has to admit, is not necessarily a good thing. Religious wars, inquisitions, persecutions, and bigotry make a macabre spectacle. Perhaps he will decide to abstain from the activities of institutional religion, as did Abraham Lincoln, who found its bickerings boresome and irrelevant to the mature mood of aspiration and wonder. Or, just the opposite, he may find an approximately satisfactory expression of his own sentiment in some existing branch of the church, perhaps that of his own family tradition. Again, he may decide that his development requires submission of unruly impulses to strong discipline, and that on the whole the historic and sacramental church is the best to tie to. In any case, the precise ecclesiastical position of the individual is not an index of the maturity of his religious sentiment. Adherence to almost any church, or to none at all, may mark those in their maturing personalities have fought through the issues of religion.

Is the test of a differentiated sentiment, then, the presence of critical tendencies? Partly yes, for a sentiment would never become differentiated unless the original stage of simple childhood belief had given way to reflective examination and questioning. But differentiation implies more than criticism; it implies an articulation and ordering of parts. There are, as we have seen, many objects, many "cognitive poles," involved in the religious orientation. The deity is a matter of concern; so too the nature of the soul, the ordering of values in life; the issues of freedom, sin, immortality; personal attitudes toward prayer, good works, creeds, tradition. The issues confronted by mature personalities are not the same in all cultures, nor in all individuals.

A differentiated organization will somehow fit all these objects into a pattern. Toward each item the individual will evolve an appropriate rational and emotional attitude, consistent with the value-structure of the sentiment. As a result the individual knows with precision his attitude toward the chief phases of theoretical doctrine and the principal issues in the moral sphere, while at the same time maintaining a genuine sense of wholeness into which the articulated parts fit.

At certain moments, those that are ordinarily called mystical, the sense of wholeness may be overwhelming. One of Freud's patients reported that for him religion was an "oceanic feeling." If the patient meant that it was always a vague gray surge and never anything else, he was describing an undifferentiated religious sentiment. In such sentiment the unconscious component is likely to be marked, and Freud would no doubt be justified in suspecting its origins to lie in a troubled sea of repression.

If, however, the patient was referring to occasional mystical states, customarily of short duration, he did well to characterize them as "oceanic." Mystical experiences yield a sense of immediacy devoid of interpretation. They are, James has said, transient, noetic, passive and ineffable.[5] One may perhaps question the attribute of ineffability in view of the ease with which some mystics have discussed the nature of these transfigured moments. A girl of fifteen tells of her first communion. During the service she had felt an increasing reverence and expectancy, and,

[5] W. James. *Op. cit.*, p. 371.

then came the holy moment in which my soul sank in the sea of love. . . . But I cannot describe in words the feeling which I then experienced. Words for it are only empty noise. There was in me such a great fullness of blessedness and of holy, pure joy. Every fiber of my feeling belonged to my Creator. At that moment I would have so liked to die. Die! O, it is no real death, it is only just the releasing of our poor body, in order that the soul thus freed may hasten back to the arms of its first Parent, its Creator.[6]

Such mystical moments differ from simple reverence in that the latter always entails some elements of interpretation. In reverence one *knows* that one is being devotional, and has an orderly and coherent chain of thoughts and feelings under voluntary control. Mysticism, on the other hand, is a benign dissociation of the stream of thought and feeling from the ordinary critical and self-conscious activities of the mind. Of course moments of reverence and moments of mysticism may be interlocked as they often are in the course of prayer.

Mystical experience is not in itself a token of a mature religious sentiment. On the other hand, it is by no means incompatible with such a sentiment. In several of its forms advanced religious thinking makes a prominent place for mystical states and invites their occurrence, sometimes regarding them as the highest attainment of religious striving. Neo-Platonism, the philosophy of Vedanta, as well as certain lines of Christian philosophy do so. They hold that the ordinary process of knowing, like desiring and valuing, requires the separation of the self (the subject) from the object of knowledge, desire or value. Such separation is inimical to the unity that religion affirms. Since the religious verity, whatever it may be, must encompass both subject and object, the distinction between them ought to be overcome. Approval is therefore given to mysticism which seeks, in complete

---

[6] O. Kupky. *Op. cit.*, p. 130. Quoted by permission of The Macmillan Company.

repose or rest in God, a state of fathomless unity, *Nirvikalpa*, able to annihilate the sense of duality and to silence the clamor of analytical interpretation. To attempt an analysis of such a state is regarded as futile and presumptuous. God is best conceived as a "nameless nothingness," the very negation of all things man can think or express. Although the cultivation of mystical states may thus be a reasonable consequence of a thoroughly mature religious outlook, or in some cases the initial cause that leads into the quest for maturity, few individuals succeed in overcoming for long the normal duality in knowing and desiring. Mysticism in its extreme form, therefore, is not an especially common form of religious functioning.

Whether or not the religion of maturity includes periods of mysticism, the basic structure of its sentiment is well differentiated, comprising many subsidiary attitudes, critically arrived at, and flexibly maintained as the sphere of experience widens.

Derivative Yet Dynamic Nature of the Mature Sentiment

The second attribute of the mature religious sentiment is found in the autonomous character of its motivational power. The energy that sustains such a sentiment may be said to pertain to it alone. For, in only slight degree, if at all, is this energy drawn from the reservoir of organic drives—from the fears, hungers, desires of the body.

It is true, as I argued in the first chapter, that the *origins* of religious life do lie, in part, in these organic cravings which, when blocked, give rise to a displaced type of longing and to transposed goals that are expressed in the language of religion. Is it then consistent to maintain, as I am now doing, that a mature religious sentiment supplies its own driving power, and becomes dynamic in its own right? Yes, I venture to assert that *the most important of all distinctions between the immature and the mature religious sentiment lies in this basic difference in their dynamic characters.*

Immature religion, whether in adult or child, is largely concerned with magical thinking, self-justification, and creature comfort. Thus it betrays its sustaining motives still to be the drives and desires of the body. By contrast, mature religion is less of a servant, and more of a master, in the economy of the life. No longer goaded and steered exclusively by impulse, fear, wish, it tends rather to control and to direct these motives toward a goal that is no longer determined by mere self-interest.

I reaffirm the point made in the first chapter, that the religious outlook is highly derivative in its origins. Born of organic unrest, of self-interested desire, of juvenile interpretation ("verbal realism"), it nonetheless undergoes extensive transformation. Like an oak tree in its growth it shatters and discards the acorn from which it originally drew nourishment. The vitality it acquires becomes authoritative over the motives from which it grew. Tracing its evolution from childhood onward, we clearly see that each stage is continuous with each other, and yet at the same time a definite emergence of new meaning and new motive is taking place.

A religious sentiment that has thus become largely independent of its origins, "functionally autonomous,"[7] cannot be regarded as a servant of other desires, even though its initial function may have been of this order. It behaves no longer like an iron filing, twisting to follow the magnet of self-centered motives; it behaves rather as a master-motive, a magnet in its own right by which other cravings are bidden to order their course. Having decided that the religious

[7] G. W. Allport. *Op. cit.*, Chapter 7.

sentiment is the best instrument for dealing with life, the self, as it were, hands over to it the task of interpreting all that comes within its view, and of providing motive power to live in accordance with an adequate frame of value and meaning, and to enlarge and energize this frame.

The power of religion to transform lives—assuming that we are dealing with genuine transformations and not with ephemeral conversions—is a consequence of the functional autonomy that marks the mature religious sentiment. Whenever this sentiment takes a prominent and active role in the personality its influence is strikingly pervasive. Many events bring it into play (the beauties of nature, the acts of men, signs of value and disvalue in everyday life), and the person's resultant response to these events is to a greater or less degree steered and determined by the religious sentiment. Perceptions and interpretations, thoughts and conduct can be thoroughly saturated by this sentiment. We know, in fact, that some stubborn and injurious forms of behavior, alcoholism for example, can hardly be transformed by anything excepting a strong, autonomous, religious sentiment.

Though the mature sentiment thus has authentic motivational character of its own, and may constitute the mainspring of life, yet it is neither fanatic nor compulsive. Fanaticism is fed by immature urgencies arising from unconscious forces that, as we have noted, enter into an uncritical, undifferentiated sentiment. Rather than admit criticism that would require the arduous process of differentiation, such a sentiment stiffens and fights intolerantly all attempts to broaden it. In compulsive religion there is a defensive ruling-out of disturbing evidence.

The absence of fanaticism in mature religion will, to some, seem a weakness. "Do not developed minds," they ask, "in the process of becoming critical and reflective, lose their glow and zeal? Does not ardor degenerate into a mere belief that certain formulas are probably true, and passion decay into an intellectualistic philosophy of religion?" Often, of course, such an entropy does occur. Sentiment may fade into nothingness. But when this happens we can be certain that religion was never a central feature of the personality. When the religious sentiment is central it characteristically keeps its ardor, and maintains throughout life an enthusiastic espousal of its objects, and an insatiable thirst for God. The degree of dynamism in the mature religious sentiment depends upon how central it is among all the various psychophysical systems that compose the personality.

The Mature Sentiment Is Consistently Directive

A third earmark of the mature sentiment lies in the consistency of its moral consequences. We have just remarked the obvious fact that, when intense, religious belief is able to transform character. While an immature sentiment is very likely to raise moral storms, and sporadically alter conduct, it lacks the steady, persistent influence of the seasoned religious outlook.

The relationship between personal religion and morality is admittedly complex. One study of contemporary college youth brings to light a striking degree of independence between the two. Many students outstanding for their sense of decency and consideration for others report that they feel no need of religion in their lives.[8] At the same time, some say that their standards of conduct, unsupported by their theological beliefs, would collapse. But on the whole, in dealing with individual cases, one is more impressed by the apparent separation of moral standards from religion than by their dependence upon it.

[8] C. W. Heath, et al. What People Are, Cambridge: Harvard University Press, 1945, pp. 42 ff.

One thinks here of the situation that came to light during the recent war. It was found that bravery, clear-headedness, emotional stability were encountered frequently among individuals brought up in religious homes but who had drifted away from the faith of their fathers. The mental and emotional stability of such "passive religionists" is high, though they now embrace no religion. Apparently what has happened is that the steadying influence of the family tradition, the discipline imposed by the parents, stemming in most cases from their own faith, combined to produce well-balanced sons. The sons are as sound as their parents or grandparents, but with a difference. They have lost faith that the standards according to which they live possess objective validity. Because of the momentum in their family tradition these young men are still in the process of "becoming," but have lost their guide in "being." Through how many generations, one may ask with Renan, can we continue to live on "the perfume of an empty vase"? Ethical standards are difficult to sustain without idealism; and idealism is difficult to sustain without a myth of Being. We often hear it said that the increase in war and crime and divorce can be traced to the decline in religious faith. And in respect to democracy itself the question has been asked: "As a form of idealism and as a standard of conduct can democracy sustain its vitality unless it is reset within the wider context of a religious sentiment that passionately affirms democracy's derivation from the Christian order?" Finally, we hear it said that the popularity of social activities in American churches is the secular residue of a religious conviction that has been lost. The vigor of the "myth in the grand style," as Oswald Spengler called it, is gone. Remaining is a mere twitch of humanitarian activity at the end of the heroic cycle.

This ominous course of reasoning cannot lightly be dismissed. At the same time it can badly exaggerate the situation that prevails. So far as social service is concerned, we are by no means justified in regarding it as a mere hollow vestige of religion. To translate the private world of thought and feeling into action is not to weaken conviction but to strengthen it. Belief in the doctrine of the person, for example, can remain firm *only* if it leads the individual to act in behalf of social betterment. So far as democracy is concerned, we cannot yet say whether its healthy growth requires metaphysical and religious support. In many lives, of course, the ideals of democracy are related to the religious sentiment. In others, this is not the case.

The principal error of the prophets of disaster is their assumption that no longer do religious sentiments generate high and consistent standards of action. This assumption is unproved. Even though in these transitional times the faith of our ancestors is not often maintained intact, yet the moral power of the religious sentiments that are formed anew in each generation is considerable. We cannot yet conclude that we are merely squandering the capital accumulated by our parents and grandparents. New religious sentiments are maturing all the time, producing fresh moral zeal, and engendering consistency upon men's purposes.

The Comprehensive Character of the Mature Sentiment

The mature mind, as we have said, demands a comprehensive philosophy of life. The hurly-burly of the world must be brought into some kind of order. And the facts calling for order are not only material; they include emotions, values, and man's strange propensity to seek his own perfection.

Casting about, the individual sees various possibilities. First of all, in this day and age he encounters humanism. Does it, he asks, succeed in binding the many-sided universe? It offers itself, in the terms of one of its advocates, as "a religion in harmony with facts as now known, recognizing nature as impersonal and inexorable, fostering cooperation under the realization that man has but himself and his fellow men upon whom to rely."[9] But humanism, he suspects, is something like science—acceptable so far as it goes, but quite uncurious regarding its own presuppositions. He doubts that the motive power for humanism is more than the lingering breeze of the powerful dynamic of Christian faith. So far as science is concerned, he knows well that his own religious faith is unlikely to rival it in clarity nor, in all points, equal it in validity; but it shall—and this is his point of insistence—it shall surpass it in *adequacy*. Religion, like philosophy, must answer questions that science dares not frame but, unlike philosophy, it must also infuse all of life with motive.

The question whether humanism may properly be called a religion is much like the question whether Communism, or any reformism, is or is not religious. Certain earmarks are identical. A cause or sincere belief of any sort, ardently embraced, performs an integrative function. It confers intelligibility and direction upon conduct, prescribes rights and duties; is highly motivational; is satisfying; and may cover all those aspects of existence that really matter to the individual. All strongly ideal interests confer unity to the mind, and provide significance and enlargement to the lives of those who possess them.

It was his perception of this fact, I believe, that led William James to circumscribe his definition of subjective religion. For him religion means "the feelings, acts, and experiences of individual men in their solitude, so far as they apprehend themselves to stand in relation to whatever they may consider the divine."[10] By thus requiring the religious sentiment to direct itself toward some conception of divinity,

[9] H. R. Rafton. Letter in the *Harvard Alumni Bulletin*, 1947, 49, p. 330.
[10] W. James. *Op. cit.*, p. 31 f.

we would probably disqualify most causes however ardently embraced. True, some zealous Communists deify Lenin, and some fanatic Nazis deify Hitler. When so, we would have, by James's definition, a true instance of religion. Whitehead's definition of religion, on the other hand, does not require a conception of the divine. For him religion is "the art and theory of the internal life of man, so far as it depends on the man himself and on what is permanent in the nature of things."[11] For James, Communism and like causes would be disqualified because they postulate no divinity; for Whitehead, because they deal only partially, if at all, with "what is permanent in the nature of things."

Approaching the matter psychologically we are bound to admit that in many lives whole-hearted zealousness for a cause acts like a religious sentiment. Such lives seem to need no other religion, for in their economy they have discovered its equivalent. Yet, even from the psychological point of view, we see that the ground covered by any secular interest, however vital, falls short of the range that characterizes a mature religious sentiment which seems never satisfied unless it is dealing with matters central to all existence. A cause may be absorbing, but it seldom includes the whole of a mature individual's horizon. Residues are left over which only religion can absorb.

The demand that one's religious sentiment be comprehensive makes for tolerance. One knows that one's life alone does not contain all possible values or all facets of meaning. Other people too have their stake in truth. The religion of maturity makes the affirmation "God is," but only the religion of immaturity will insist, "God is precisely what I say He is." The Hindu Vedas were speaking mature language when they asserted, "Truth is one; men call it by many names."

[11] A. N. Whitehead. *Religion in the Making*, New York: Macmillan, 1926, p. 16.

Integral Nature of the Mature Sentiment

Closely allied to the demand for comprehensiveness is the mature individual's insistence that his religious sentiment compose a homogeneous pattern. Not only must its coverage be great but its design must be harmonious. Like a tapestry weaver he is forced to work behind the design he creates. Holding the threads singly and inserting them with care he can only hope that the pattern he fashions will be whole when seen from the front. From behind the loom the complexity of strands appears baffling. To fashion an integral pattern is the task of a lifetime—and more.

A modern man, brought up in the Hebraic-Christian tradition, finds that the theology and ethics of this tradition were written down in an era that was pre-scientific and pre-technological. Bucolic parables belong to a mode of life remote from our own. Commandments and codes formulated in an age of shepherds and petty kings seem difficult to implement in an age of giant industry, instant communication, and atomic energy. Since we cannot and will not turn our backs on the modern world, then the religion we embrace cannot be pre-scientific; nor anti-scientific; it must be co-scientific. But science alone produces none of the integrity, the direction, or the zeal, that are needed in order to assure the benefits of its own achievements. It is up to modern man, the weaver, to take the strands of science and bind them with values and purpose. No threads may be rejected, perhaps least of all those that come from modern psychology, psychiatry, and psychoanalysis. For to apply the prophetic teachings of past ages to a technical age requires special assistance from the sciences that deal with personality and with human relations.

To be truly integral a religious sentiment must admit the disturbing fact that human conduct, to a large degree, is determined. To ascribe more freedom of will to man than he possesses is to hold to an anachronism and to destroy the hope for a proper integration of science and religion. Yet an adroit mind will readily perceive that the degree and type of freedom a man has depends in part upon what he believes. If he thinks he is hopelessly bound he will not exert himself, and if he fails to exert himself he will not improve his lot. If, on the contrary, he believes that there are doors that may be opened and that lead to a fuller realization of values, he will explore, discover, enter. A well-differentiated religious sentiment engenders freedom simply because the possessor of such a sentiment finds that obdurate though nature and habit may be, still there are regions where aspiration, effort, and prayer are efficacious. A person believing he is free uses what equipment he has more flexibly and successfully than does the person who is convinced he dwells in chains.

An integral sentiment will have difficulty in accommodating the problem of evil. It is upon this rock, and upon the reefs of determinism, that most religious sentiments are wrecked in their quest for maturity. I shall not attempt to review all the solutions to the problem of evil that struggle for a place in the mature mind. A solution acceptable to one individual may be unacceptable to another. One holds that the only way out is to regard God himself as a finite Being, suffering from dark spots in His own nature and unable to control the tides of natural law and of man's perverseness. Another, while professing inability to solve the issue, holds fast to the conviction that religion, effectively applied, would eliminate at least the evil that stems from human ignorance and misconduct. Another says that our understanding is inadequate, that what we call evil is a stage in development. Were the veil of Maya destroyed the essential virtue of all things would appear. "My thoughts are not your thoughts, neither are your ways my way, saith the Lord." However the problem is handled, the suffering of innocent persons is for most people the hardest of all facts to integrate into a religious sentiment. Yet the issue has to be faced and fought through; otherwise, the sentiment cannot become mature.

Heuristic Character of the Mature Sentiment

The final attribute of mature religion is its essentially heuristic character. An heuristic belief is one that is held tentatively until it can be confirmed or until it helps us discover a more valid belief. For example, the individual fashions his creed and conceives his deity as best he can. Perhaps he accepts the authority of some revelation. If so, he does it not because he can demonstrate its final validity by events occurring in time and space, but because that which he accepts helps him find out better and fuller answers to the questions that perplex him. His faith is his working hypothesis. He knows perfectly well that doubt concerning it is still theoretically possible.

It is characteristic of the mature mind that it can act whole-heartedly even without absolute certainty. It can be sure without being cocksure. We are not positive that we shall be alive tomorrow but it is a good hypothesis to proceed on. We are not certain that the social agencies of our big cities are decreasing the margin of suffering and evil in our midst, but it seems like a probability worth backing. It is still less demonstrable that you and I will succeed in the goals we have respectively set for ourselves; but it is the mere chance of success that nerves us for sustained and eager endeavor. The odds of success do not have to be large in order to keep us going. Writers as diverse in stripe as Descartes, Pascal, Newman, James, have made the point. Faith is a risk, but everyone in some way or other is bound to take it.

Probabilities always guide our lives. Sometimes the degree of statitsical probability can be ascertained; more often, as in the area of religion, it cannot. It is not necessary to know how probable a probability is in order to embrace it. In religion, according to Cardinal Newman:

It is faith and love which give to probability a force which it has not in itself. Faith and love are directed toward an object; in the vision of that object they live; it is that object, received in faith and love, which renders it reasonable to take probability as sufficient for internal conviction.[12]

Newman goes on to say that though *certainty* is impossible, the commitment one makes—a fusion of probability, faith and love—engenders sufficient *certitude* for the guidance of one's life.

Such a commitment, even when it is tentatively held, has important consequences. For all accomplishment results from taking risks in advance of certainties. Chronic skepticism, inhibitory and depressive thoughts, are incompatible with everything excepting vegetative existence. The optimistic bias toward life is a necessary condition for life. Only by having expectations of consequences beyond the limits of certainty do we make these consequences more likely to occur. Faith engenders the energy which when applied to the task in hand enhances the probability of success.

What many unbelievers do not realize is that the mature believer's eyes are wide open. The latter knows that he is finally uncertain of his ground. But he feels, reasonably enough, that in a world where optimistic bias and faith are largely responsible for human accomplishment, it would be silly for him to lapse into unproductive skepticism, so long as he has a chance of being correct. The believer is often closer to the agnostic than we think. Both, with equal candor,

---

[12] J. H. Newman. *Apologia pro Vita sua*, New York: E. P. Dutton (Everyman's Library), 1912, p. 43.

may concede that the nature of Being cannot be known; but the believer, banking on a probability, slight though he may deem it to be, finds that the energy engendered and the values conserved prove the superiority of affirmation over indecisiveness.

We may then say that the mature religious sentiment is ordinarily fashioned in the workshop of doubt. Though it has known intimately "the dark night of the soul," it has decided that theoretical skepticism is not incompatible with practical absolutism. While it knows all the grounds for skepticism, it serenely affirms its wager. In so doing, it finds that the successive acts of commitment, with their beneficent consequences, slowly strengthen the faith and cause the moments of doubt gradually to disappear.

Some people, of course, say they are unable to entertain religious propositions with less than full certainty—even though these same people commit themselves gladly to the probabilities of everyday life. They seem to fear that unless one has certainty one will lose the vital force to proceed. Their dilemma is like that stated by opponents of liberal education: How, they ask, can we allow full play to analysis and criticism, and still expect our youth to develop firm purpose, strong character, and devotion to a right cause? There are others, Renan and Eugene O'Neill among them, who go further and insist that belief in an *illusion* is necessary in order to sustain purpose. I think we need not worry unduly about the matter. To the genuinely mature personality a full-faced view of reality in its grimmest aspects is not incompatible with an heuristic-commitment that has the power to turn desperation into active purpose. An heuristic-commitment is not a matter of illusion, at least until such a time as the probabilities upon which it is based are proved to be absolutely groundless. And if one cannot prove the religious commitment to rest on certainties, neither can one prove it to be groundless.

Conscience and Mental Health

PSYCHIATRY AND RELIGION both see man as a far from perfect being. For centuries religion has endeavored to improve the situation. Psychiatry has only recently entered the lists, and its youthful vigor raises new hope. Each recent decade seems to have chalked up gains. In the 1880's, Charcot founded medical psychotherapy. Previously, Pinel and Dorothea Dix had helped to dispel the dark retributive theory of mental disorder. In the 1890's, Kraepelin devised a diagnostic classification for the major mental diseases. In the next decade, the mental hygiene movement was launched. In the next, the Freudian revolution overspread the psychological world. In the 1920's, among other advances, the ingenious fever treatment for general paresis was discovered, making curable what was previously considered a fatal form of insanity. During the 1930's, psychosomatic medicine developed, based upon the explicit recognition of the all-important fact that what a man believes profoundly affects his health, both mental and physical. In the recent decade, including the war years, all of these gains have been consolidated, together with new discoveries concerning the value of convulsive and other shock therapies, and of brain surgery.

These strides have brightened man's outlook to such an

extent that he now refuses to face the pain and suffering of mental difficulties with resignation. He expects science to diminish this domain of human misery just as it has so brilliantly reduced the region of physical distress. Year by year mental hygiene takes a position of greater prominence in the schools, in the pulpits, in the press, on the bookstands. Mental health is clearly our goal. Psychology and religion are two acceptable means, but it is generally expected that religion must abet and never oppose psychological science.

How Successful Is Psychotherapy?

Clearly we are undergoing a great ideational revolution. But the achievements of this revolution are not yet conclusively favorable. Mental disease has not diminished; rather it has increased, at least among the older third of the population. In the American states with the best hospital facilities, it is now estimated that one person in ten will receive institutional care for mental ailment some time during his life.[1] We know too that in recent times social disorganization in the guise of war, mass persecutions, divorce, delinquency, show upward rather than downward trends. The suffering of individuals has not lessened, but has been bitterly aggravated. Hence, statistically viewed, the success of modern psychotherapy has been up to now not merely negligible but negative.

One properly replies, of course, that the environmental conditions, so important to mental health, are not the responsibility of psychotherapy, as this discipline is now conceived. It would be foolish to blame psychiatrists for the ravages of economic depression, war, social upheaval. It is

[1] C. Landis and J. D. Page. *Modern Society and Mental Disease*, New York: Farrar and Rinehart, 1938.

not psychiatry, but the sciences of government, of sociology, of human relations that have overslept. If the psychiatrist is at fault at all, it is because he does not see clearly enough that mental health and disease are to a considerable extent dependent upon the social setting. Working in isolation he can never solve problems that require concerted effort. Widespread improvement in mental health awaits the time when he can work effectively with statesmen, sociologists, the clergy, educators, anthropologists, economists, social workers, administrators, psychologists, and medical practitioners.

The psychiatrist, although he is himself a physician, receives less support from other physicians than he is entitled to expect. Few medical men realize fully the truth that what the patient believes profoundly affects his health. Untrained in psychology, in psychiatry, in psychosomatic medicine, and bewildered by the irrational troubles of their patients, physicians often prefer to treat ailing organs rather than ailing persons. The modern hospitals in which they labor are usually well stocked with laboratory, radiological, surgical equipment, but with little or nothing for the human mind. Recently I visited a public health hospital specializing in stomach ailments, 75 per cent of which were regarded by the chief medical officer as psychogenic. Yet this hospital, in all other ways admirably equipped, had nothing for the mind—excepting one isolated padded cell.

In one other respect, though this time innocently, medical science is responsible for the present critical state of affairs. In the process of lengthening the average human life by many years medicine has bestowed just that much more time upon the average person for the development of mental difficulties. Prolonging life is a dubious blessing indeed to those who will develop serious mental disorders that they would otherwise have been spared.

Psychotherapy, for all the progress it has made, is still a

young art. Practitioners are few. The techniques of treatment are not yet well tested. A few devices, like sedation, shock, or surgery, are technically specialized. But for the most part psychotherapists employ implements borrowed from the clergy. The reason is simple enough: until recent times the church alone dealt with troubles of personality. The borrowed devices include listening, encouragement, advice, and the relationship of transference wherein the applicant finds security in dependence upon his counselor. Historically the church has employed also the Sacrament of Penance, and although the ritual of the confessional is certainly different from the ritual of the analyst's couch, the element of similarity is still apparent.

Psychotherapy and Religion

If the therapist's techniques are in the main so similar to the pastor's, why is the cure of souls gravitating and more out of the hands of the church and into the hands of psychiatrists? There are several reasons. For one thing, people prefer to look for physical causes of their difficulties, and the psychiatrist, being a medical man, may find such a cause. If he does, then the patient is saved from the necessity of facing up to the realities of his inner life. A cause in the body is less disturbing than a cause in one's character. The pastor, he fears, will not sense the possible physical basis for his trouble, but may confuse mental, physical, and moral aspects in a manner that will be humiliating. The pastor, he fears, may at inappropriate moments preach or pray or pass moral judgment. Further, the vast prestige of modern science mantles the psychiatrist, and the patient approaches him with high hopes, thinking no doubt of the spectacular achievements of contemporary medicine. He feels that psychotherapists, unlike the clergy, keep up to date with such discoveries about the human mind as are being made. Finally, he is not uninfluenced by the united front presented by science in contrast to the divided sects of religion.[2]

Since all these considerations are cogent and reasonable we could—but for one fact—conclude that the drift to psychiatry is altogether proper and desirable. The modern mind might easily decide, "Here is a new branch of science. God, if there be a God, has shown that He chooses to work by natural laws alone. Just as natural history has forsaken the confines of sacred literature and passed wholly into the hands of natural science, so should problems of mental history and functioning pass into the hands of the newer psychological science." The single fact that weighs against this wholly secular solution is the ever insistent truth that what a man believes to a large extent determines his mental and physical health. What he believes about his business, his associates, his wife, his immediate future, is important; even more so, what he believes about life in general, its purpose and design. Religious belief, simply because it deals with fundamentals, often turns out to be the most important belief of all.

Some psychiatrists freely acknowledge this fact. One, an unbeliever, remarked that when he finds religion present in a patient he never disturbs it, for in the long run it is likely to turn out to be the leading factor in the cure. Some therapists today incline to see in almost every neurosis an unsolved metaphysical issue. Jung's oft-cited statement is to the effect that of his thousands of patients over the age of thirty-five, "all have been people whose problem in the last resort was that of finding a religious outlook on life."[3]

[2] Cf. C. Landis. Psychotherapy and religion, *Review of Religion*, 1946, 10, 413–424.
[3] C. G. Jung. *Modern Man in Search of a Soul*, New York: Harcourt, Brace and Co., 1933.

Religion and therapy are alike in their insistence upon the need for greater unification and order in personality. Both recognize that the healthy mind requires an hierarchical organization of sentiments, ordinarily with one master-sentiment holding the dominant position. Psychotherapy does not insist that the strong central interest should be religious in character, although this possibility, as I have just said, is ordinarily recognized and respected. But from the point of view of psychotherapy sentiments dealing with family, art, sports, business, would be equally good if they succeeded in marshaling energy and bestowing order in the life. Religion is bound to disagree at this point, asking whether such sentiments are adequate to sustain personality. Can a person ever really attain integration until he has likewise signed and sealed a treaty of peace with the cosmos?

A certain psychiatrist requires the patients in his private sanitarium to attend and companion those who are more ill than they. Such activity, he finds, has a markedly integrative effect, re-deploying and re-centering the energies that were harmfully spent in self-pity, in resentment, in fantasy. The fact that health flows from the practice of the Christian virtue of charity is of no particular concern to this psychiatrist. To him the practice of charity is just one constructive interest capable of knitting together the broken personalities of his patients. The religionist, however, would maintain that the gain is far from accidental. Love—incomparably the greatest psychotherapeutic agent—is something that professional psychiatry cannot of itself create, focus, nor release.

It is well to be clear about this matter. Psychological science, in which psychotherapy is rooted, finds itself at a disadvantage in dealing with the phenomena of human affiliation. It has little to say about man's desire for loving attachment. Dr. Suttie, a British psychiatrist, has rightly observed that modern science represents a "flight from tenderness," and thus stands in antithesis to religion which seeks above all else to affirm and establish tender relationships.[4]

The principal reason for this flight lies, I think, in the essentially analytical nature of science. Of necessity it deals with salient figures abstracted from encompassing grounds. Of the *underlying* properties of biological and social life it has little to say. The demand and capacity for tenderness and for symbiotic relationship are always with us, and for that very reason they cannot be clearly analyzed.

It would be instructive to measure the space given by modern dynamic psychology to hostility, aggression, rivalry, power, and anxiety; and to compare this accumulation with the microscopic amount of space devoted to the friendly attachments in human relationships. Negative and hostile phenomena stand out prominently simply because they are regarded as alien intrusions into the original and normal ground of human trust. It is fear and hate that we regard as problems, not love and affiliation. What claims our attention is the array of reactive phenomena that result from love-deprivation.

We are in danger of forgetting that these negative states, always prominent in mental disorder, are secondary developments. They come about when the groundwork of life is disturbed. We know, for example, that in infants, behavior disorders commonly follow interruptions of the original symbiotic relationship between the child and its mother. The child who feels himself to be rejected can be counted on to develop a mental health problem. So too can an adult. The security that comes from being loved and from giving love is the groundwork for wholesome existence at any age of life.

Psychotherapy knows the healing power of love, but finds

[4] I. D. Suttie. *The Origins of Love and Hate*, London: Kegan Paul, Trench, Trubner & Co., 1935, p. 2.

itself unable to do much about it. On the side of theory, as I have just said, it lacks an adequate concept of the nature of tenderness. On the side of practice, the psychotherapist finds himself unable to supply the love his patient needs, nor to receive the love the patient wants to give. The normal stage of "transference" in the course of treatment betrays this need, but it is a temporary step. Transference must be broken. As for mental hospitals, they seem equipped to give their inmates almost everything they require excepting love.

By contrast, religion—especially the Christian religion—offers an interpretation of life and a rule of life based wholly upon love. It calls attention again and again to this fundamental groundwork. On love for God and man "hang all the Law and the Prophets." The emphasis is insistent: "Beloved, let us love one another: for love is of God; and everyone that loveth is born of God, and knoweth God. He that loveth not knoweth not God; for God is love." (I St. John, iv, 7–8.)

Perhaps the very insistence of religion in this matter is in part responsible for the "tenderness tabu" that has descended upon psychology. Having rejected the religious approach to the cure of souls, science regards it as more realistic to center attention upon the reactive conditions of the mind—upon hate, aggression, compulsive sexuality—even if these are merely the pathological conditions due to deprivation of love.

Perhaps a shift in emphasis is now coming about. In recent years psychologists have stressed more and more the unconditional need of the child for security and love within the home. I think we can now discern an extension of this principle to the adult who, at bottom, is now recognized as having a passionate hunger for affiliation with his family, his coworkers, and his community. True, it is still rare to find a therapist who sees health-giving significance in the concept of "love of God." Yet to many people a sense of cosmic affiliation is needed to round out and order the sum-total of their attachments. Love of God is needed in order to make life seem complete, intelligible, right.

Religion, we conclude, is superior to psychotherapy in the allowance it makes for the affiliative need in human nature. But when it comes to a question of implementing this insight we are confronted by the age-long failure of religion to turn doctrine into practice. More and more people seem impatient with the shortcomings of unacted religious profession. A host of accusations arise.

Some critics argue that religion at best is a namby-pamby suggestion therapy, providing blinders for some, patches and crutches for others. Suggestion therapy, they argue, does little excepting anaesthetize the individual to the starkly realistic problems confronting him. They add, correctly enough, that unless a person can face the deeply pessimistic elements in his situation he is not likely to solve his problems either with psychotherapy or religion. In support of their argument these critics point to the shoppers who wander from one religious cult to another, learning here, that their problems are illusory; there, that should listen for the "vibrations"; and elsewhere, that in the world to come there will be fish fries and dancing. Yet the critics fail to perceive that it is only religious immaturity that seeks suggestive therapy of this sort. A mature religious sentiment is neither escapist nor evasive.

One sometimes hears that preoccupation with religion engenders mental disorder. For evidence, they point to the large number of disturbed people, especially schizophrenic and depressed patients, who suffer from theopathic delusions, rationalizing their misery with fantastic religious formulae. Isn't it obvious in these cases that preoccupation with religion constitutes an obstacle, rather than an aid, to health? To answer this particular question a careful study of the history of cases showing religious obsession should be made. Pending such an investigation, a contrary hypothesis seems equally reasonable. When people feel utterly strange and out of touch with their environment they cast around desperately for an explanation of their peculiar feelings. It may well turn out that preoccupation with religion was not the cause but the *effect* of the breakdown. What language other than religious can represent to a disturbed patient the mysterious forces that he feels? When imagination and emotion run wild, the symbols of religion seem most nearly adequate to the task of rationalization that faces any patient suffering from a catastrophic change in personality.

Our critic still persists. Are not many religious leaders clearly borderline psychotics? Yes, history indicates that some mystics and reformers suffered marked instability. St. Ignatius, Luther, St. Theresa, Fox, Wesley, come to mind. The correlation, however, is probably not significant, for it seems to hold equally true of inventors, literary geniuses, statesmen. Unless one deviates in mental type from the prevailing norm, one can scarcely be creative or describe new horizons.

An important concept in modern therapy is that of shock. Sufferers who are tangled up with worries and misgivings seem often to need a jolt to pry them loose from their chains of misery. Since most people have been brought up with religious ideas of some sort, they may need to be shaken free from their infantile preconceptions. In psychotherapy today we find electric shocks, pharmacological shocks, and psychological shocks. It is not commonly enough recognized that psychoanalysis is in part a form of psychological shock treatment. Culturally, it was the shocking *coupe de grâce* to the Victorian age. Individually, it is the shocking discovery of hates, fears, lusts, that have lain repressed in the caverns of unconsciousness. The psychoanalytic process drags into the light of day the noisome inhabitants of these caverns. The patient finds himself, with considerable relief, thinking and uttering shocking ideas, sometimes lewd, sometimes blasphemous. He experiences a new freedom in shifting from infantile credulousness to more adult incredulity. Feeling secure with his analyst, he dares to attack the rigidity of his own conscience, and to tumble the idols of his own infancy. Such mental rioting is purging in its effect, startling and relieving. A slum must be razed before a new and suitable edifice can be erected.

Certain questions, however, are in order concerning this type of psychological shock treatment. Does the patient, thus relieved, feel more at home in the universe? Delivered from a sense of confusion, has he found a new order? Liberated from untenable values, has he found more solid values? Losing infantile restrictions, has he attained adult purposes? Sometimes these gains do come, if not in the course of the analysis, then often in the subsequent period. In such instances the analysis has justified itself; in other instances it may be actively harmful. Sometimes psychotherapists are more deft in destroying the old than in helping to build the new.

It is certainly true that in the current vocabulary of psychological science many people find fresh insights. In particular the new and startling language of psychoanalysis enables many a mind to shake itself free from immature conceptions of duty, guilt, danger. It is here that an interesting possibility suggests itself for our generation. Might young people, brought up in the symbolism and faith of psychoanalysis, when confronted by life's perplexities, find the less familiar but more heroic expressions of the world's great religions fresh and insightful, and more germane to the totality of their experience? If therapy for minds in distress requires a reorientation of perspective, it may well turn out that the historic religious conceptions of good and evil have a special merit for modern minds caught in the web of psychological terminology.

Returning to the relation of the clergyman and psychiatrist, this conclusion seems in order: insofar as the clergy is the better able to deal with issues of basic belief, values, and orientation toward life, he has an inescapable role to play in the conservation and advancement of mental health. His role seems complementary to that of the psychoanalyst who, by professional training, is ordinarily more skillful in plowing than in planting. But insofar as modern psychotherapeutic techniques have become medically oriented, or otherwise specialized, the clergyman, of course, must give ground. No longer does the cure of souls fall entirely to his office. The growth of psychological science does not mean, however, that he is relieved of responsibility. Quite the contrary: it means that now for the first time he can embrace his ministry to the individual with some degree of confidence, for he no longer stands alone in the face of a task too great for his skill and training. He can make psychological science his ally, and share with its practitioners the solution of a problem of joint concern. Furthermore, he can and should become familiar with many of the psychological procedures that may fortify his own skills. Within the past few years over one thousand clergymen have received clinical training in hospital centers where special institutes have been conducted for their benefit.[5]

Pastoral-psychiatric teamwork is a rapidly expanding conception. As with many teams it is necessary for one member to be more flexible and adaptable than the other, in order that the relationship may run smoothly. It seems likely that the clergy and the theological schools for the present will have to be the suitor, the planner, the adaptor, until the team is strongly established. We note the vigorous disposi-

---

[5] An organ of the movement for clinical training of the clergy is the *Journal of Pastoral Care*, with offices at Andover Hall, Cambridge, Massachusetts.

tion or the part of the clergy to include psychology in their program of training. Not yet do psychiatrists seem to sense their need for the inclusion of philosophy and theology in their preparation for practice.

Conflict and Conscience

Mental ailments, whether major or minor in degree, are reflections of conflict within the personality. Often there are hereditary or physical factors underlying this conflict, especially in certain severe conditions of mental disorder. But whether or not our difficulties have a biogenetic basis they always betray a clash of contradictory impulses.

In stating this fact the vocabulary of religion and of modern science differ markedly, though their meanings are essentially the same. The religious vocabulary seems dignified but archaic; our scientific vocabulary, persuasive but barbaric. "His Id and super-ego have not learned to cooperate," writes the modern mental hygienist; "The flesh lusteth contrary to the spirit, and the spirit to the flesh," writes St. Paul. "Feelings of guilt suggest poor personality teamwork," says the twentieth-century specialist; "Purify your hearts, ye double-minded," exhorts St. James. "The capacity of the ego to ward off anxiety is enlarged if the ego has considerable affection for his fellows and a positive goal to help them." Correspondingly, St. John writes, "Perfect love casteth out fear." It would be difficult, I suspect, to find any proposition in modern mental hygiene that has not been expressed with venerable symbols in some portion of the world's religious literature.

Most of the conflicts that cause damage to mental health—and here again psychology and religion agree—have to do with courses of conduct the individual regards as impulsively desirable and those he regards as morally obligatory. Whether we call it conscience or super-ego, the moral sense is almost always involved in any serious conflict. The consequences of violating conscience have traditionally been called "sin." The consequences of violating the super-ego are known in modern parlance as "guilt feelings." The parallel is still close.

One of the most significant features of modern mental hygiene is its attempt to make a scientific analysis of the nature of conscience. The first question asked is whether conscience is inborn. The best scientific answer seems to be No—in one sense, Yes—in another. Quite clearly *specific ideas* of what is right and wrong are not innate. Cultures are too variable; individuals are too variable. To honor the Sabbath Day is not an injunction to trouble the primitive Hawaiian conscience. Nor is the sin the Hawaiian feels at eating standing on his feet a source of concern to the Christian conscience. The cultural relativity of conscience is marked, but even so, the case may have been overstated by anthropologists. It is a matter calling for more study, particularly today when it is vital to know just how much moral agreement there is among the peoples of the world. In spite of differing tabus and imperatives, it seems that all peoples prize kindness to children, loyalty to the in-group, and they have a not wholly capricious sense of justice. We cannot yet be too sure that the content of human conscience is endlessly varied.

A further argument against the innateness of conscience comes from the fact that one can observe the child's predicament during the slow and awkward process of furnishing his conscience. We see the parent, using rewards and punishments, repetition and emphasis, trying to teach the child what is right and what is wrong. The process, we perceive, is painstaking and difficult. Even in adolescence, we note, the young person prefers to have external authority regulate his conduct. He wants leadership, authority. It is difficult to interiorize the backbone. This obvious dependence on learning, and the lateness with which the mature conscience is formed, make it certain that conscience is not furnished at birth.

At the same time, it is equally evident that the *capacity* for conscience exists in nearly every person. In the course of social living the individual is bound to form a conscience. Only in the very exceptional cases of what Lombroso called moral imbecility, and modern science sometimes calls "psychopathy," do feelings of right and wrong seem absent.

Conscience is astonishingly universal, and is by no means a product of the Christian tradition, certainly not of Puritanism. In all religions we find sin, contrition, and appeal for forgiveness playing a prominent part. A Babylonian prayer of four thousand years ago reveals an acutely sensitive conscience:

Oh my God, my transgressions are very great, very great my sins. I transgress and know it not. I wander on wrong paths and know it not. I am silent and in tears and none takes me by the hand. My God, who knowest the unknown, be merciful. In the midst of the stormy waters come to my assistance, take me by the hand.[6]

Important facts about conscience are, then, its universality in the human race (excepting in rare pathological instances), the variability of its dictates with cultural standards (though this variability may be currently overestimated), and the slow and frequently painful way in which it is acquired through the processes of learning in childhood and adolescence. Now we need to guard against a common misconception to which these facts sometimes lead.

If we are unwary we are likely to say that conscience is

[6] Abridged from M. Jastrow. *Religion of Babylonia and Assyria*, Boston: Ginn & Co., 1898, p. 321.

the lingering vestige of parental coercion and childhood fear. We observe how the young child is warned that he "must not" strike his baby sister, that he "must" form habits of modesty. The teaching, we note, is often enforced by punishment or threat. The child cannot be expected to know *why* he must perform some acts and avoid others. The sanctions to him are a blur. In some cases parental punishment descends if he disobeys; in others he finds that nature does the retaliating when he violates its laws; in others the penalty turns out to be social ostracism or even a brush with the police; in still others, he feels a vague sanction of divine wrath hovering over him. In no case can the reasons for good and acceptable conduct be fully understood by the child. In all, the sanctions to him seem confused and wholly external. His super-ego is a troublesome baggage of parental injunctions.

But later (how much later depends on the person) the sanctions become internal, and are based upon a sense of "ought" rather than "must." In maturity, and even well before, a sharp distinction grows up between the feeling of "must" and of "ought." I "must" buy some new shoes, but there is no moral obligation to do so. I "must" get some gas for my car, but there is no "ought" involved. On the other hand, I "ought" to write a letter, but I am under no coercion to do so. I "ought" to make the best possible choices in my life, but no one excepting myself will insist. My discomfort when I violate my sense of "ought" is a discomfort wholly apart from my fear of physical sanctions I incur if I violate nature's or society's laws.[7]

The transformation from the sense of "ought" is due only in part to the internalizing of the teaching received in childhood. Not everything that was once a "must" of the super-

[7] For a fuller discussion of this important distinction see P. Bertocci, A reinterpretation of moral obligation, *Philosophy and Phenomenological Research*, 1945, 6, 270–283.

ego becomes an "ought" of the mature conscience. The latter no longer depends upon the enforced teaching of parent or nurse, but upon the values that maturity holds—and in most respects these differ sharply from the values of early childhood. Psychotherapists, it is true, sometimes discover troublesome vestiges of infantile conscience plaguing mature life. But their very concern with these vestiges proves that adult conscience is expected to have adult stature and to escape entirely from the habit-structure of early childhood. Like all other ingredients of personality, conscience is expected to keep pace with the individual's age and experience. It helps to relate the person to reality as he now conceives it. It is a *present* guide to conduct, and as such, serves an important function in the economy and health of an adult life. Hence in the normal personality it may *not* be viewed as a carry-over from childhood, a parentally imposed super-ego. Functionally autonomous of its roots, it is now arbiter of adult values.

Conscience should not be reified. It is not a "man within the breast," nor is it a separate department of personality. Rather it is the knife-edge that all our values press upon us whenever we are acting, or have acted, contrary to these values. Conscience is by no means exclusively a religious phenomenon. We know many irreligious people who have acute consciences. For individuals with a civic sentiment, these is a corresponding civic conscience. When one's professional acts do not agree with one's professional sentiment, the professional conscience is pricked. A scientist has a scientific conscience; an artist, an artistic conscience; the underworld has its own strict code whose violation may awaken the still small voice even when transgressions against the larger code of society do not. Conscience is the indicator of the measure of agreement between our conduct and our values, whatever they be.

If conscience should not be reified, neither should it be fragmented. When we speak of a social conscience, a professional conscience, a religious conscience, we do not mean that each person has an indefinite number of separate sensitizers. There is as much unity of conscience as there is unity of personality. In a well-organized life the sentiment structure is not in conflict, neither are the dictates of conscience. A hierarchical organization prevents intolerable jangles. As if further to diminish discord, our keenest feelings of guilt are prompted only by violations of the highest sentiments in our personal hierarchy. Conduct out of line with a minor sentiment troubles us little, while deviations from the principal highway of our lives are marked by a sense of guilt, provided, of course, these deviations are felt to be willful and not due merely to the force of circumstances over which we have no control.

In the interests of mental health it is essential that conscience be as mature as the master-sentiments to which it corresponds. Its functioning must depend not upon what happened in childhood, but upon the contemporary character of the sentiment. Hence it is necessary for the mature conscience to distinguish between truly adult and juvenile issues. If it does not do so, inappropriate vestiges of infantile guilt may haunt the individual. Sometimes the services of a psychotherapist are required in order to remove these lingering infantilisms, and to free the individual so that he may refashion his conscience to accord with his mature values at a mature level.[8]

[8] The distinction between an immature and a mature conscience is helpfully discussed by Erich Fromm in *Man for Himself*, New York: Rinehart & Company, 1947. The mark of an immature conscience, says Fromm, is its authoritarian nature. It is ridden by a sense of obedience, self-sacrifice, duty, and resignation. The victim fears to lose the approval of the father figure (the Führer, the priest, the deity) who dominates an essentially childish super-ego. By contrast, the mature conscience is animated by adult sentiments, by self-chosen goals, by a continuously productive relation between the individual and his surrounding world.

Excepting for one feature of his analysis I would subscribe whole-

Since in many lives the religious sentiment is prominent, and since it has by its very nature extraordinarily wide scope —touching most facets of personal and social conduct—it is natural that conscience and religion should in our minds be frequently confused. But as we have seen, irreligious people may, and usually do, have lively consciences of their own. And on the other hand, many features of the religious sentiment have no direct relation to conscience. Adoration, trust, understanding, a sense of peace, and many other religious states of mind, involve no moral aspect at all. The burglar alarm in a bank vault is but one feature of a complex security system. It is activated when the system is violated. So it is with conscience, which normally acts only when the integrity of the sentiment is threatened by conduct incompatible with its essential structure. The alarm is normally silent, but when it sounds the maintenance of integration requires that it be heeded.

Aspects of Integration

Psychology's chief contribution to mental health is the concept of integration, a term less Biblical, but meaning

---

heartedly to Fromm's position. He mistakenly assumes that a religious conscience, almost of necessity, is an authoritarian (immature) conscience. While he is right in pointing out that great religions have a way of turning into power systems that seize control of the youthful adherent's conscience, he fails to see that this control may be only temporary. The individual in his course of maturing may *rediscover* for himself the essential truths of his religion, and thus incorporate them into a wholly productive and rational conscience. The fact that Christian doctrine, for example, may be accepted in a supine manner by some people, neither invalidates the doctrine nor prevents its wholehearted acceptance by an individual who in the course of his quest discovers its relevance to the totality of his own life-experience. It does not follow, therefore, as Fromm concludes, that the only mature ethics must be a humanistic ethics.

much the same as St. James's "single-mindedness."[9] Integration means the forging of approximate mental unity out of discordant impulses and aspirations. No one can say, "I will integrate my life," and expect to find it done. For the most part integration is a by-product of various favorable techniques of living. Perfect integration, of course, is never achieved, but to be even reasonably successful it must, as we have seen, admit the requirements of the mature conscience. All strongly ideal interests, we know, tend to unify the mind. But in principle, the religious interest, being most comprehensive, is best able to serve as an integrative agent.

Another road favorable to integration is humor, man's principal technique for getting rid of irrelevancies. His laughter disposes of much that is unpredicted, capricious, and misfit in his life. Humor may throw an otherwise intolerable situation into a new and manageable perspective. The neurotic who learns to laugh at himself may be on the way to self-management, perhaps to cure.

On the face of it humor seems antithetical to religion. The virtue of religion is sincerity; the virtue of humor is insincerity. Humor says essentially that nothing really matters, for basically the universe is comic. If God made it, He was certainly absent-minded. Religion says something does matter in the last analysis; all important things at bottom are congruous. Humor pushed to its extreme is cynicism, and as such is not compatible with true integration of personality. Comical pluralism could shred a life into hilarious fragments. Yet the opposition is not irreconcilable. Religion takes up where humor leaves off. Having decided that there is some-

[9] Among theological writers especially interested in the bearing of religion upon the psychological process of integration are Swedenborg (see H. D. Spoerl. Critical Points in Regeneration, *The New Christianity*, 1946, 12, 62–72), and S. Kierkegaard (see especially his *Purity of Heart Is to Will One Thing*, New York: Harper & Bros., transl. 1938).

thing beyond laughter, a core of life that is "solemn, serious, tender," there yet remains plenty of clear room for jesting. For to the religious person, as well as for the irreligious, the design of the universe is by no means apparent at all times, and its *non-sequiturs*, its "mechanical inelasticities" are fair game for laughter—so long as the ultimate direction of one's life-intention is fixed. Humor helps to integrate personality by disposing of all conflicts that do not really matter.

Integration does not require a completed view of life. In fact, completed achievements leave us hollow and at loose ends. It is only the unfinished tasks that integrate and motivate. Perceiving this fact, Goethe insisted that personal salvation lies always in the striving to achieve, never in mere attainment. You recall Faust's wager with Mephisto. If ever in the course of life's quest Faust—the epic prototype of Man—should be satisfied, should say, "Hold, thou art so fair," then might Mephisto take his soul. But it was Faust, with his insatiable hunger for more and more experience and knowledge, who won the wager and with it his salvation. That which is ever not quite fulfilled is best able to hold the attention, guide effort, and maintain unity. It is for this reason that religion qualifies as an integrative agent *par excellence*. Precisely because religious accomplishment is always incomplete, its cementing character in the personal life is therefore all the greater.

Integration is often hindered by direct, grimly determined effort. The Nancy school of psychiatrics noted that often the effort to keep from doing a wrong thing seems to magnify our chances of doing that very thing. They designated this tendency the "law of reversed effect." Many years earlier St. Paul had discovered the same principle: "I find then a law that, when I would do good, evil is present with me" (Romans 7:21). Tense moral struggles, says psychotherapy, require most of all relaxation. They require surrender, says religion—give God a chance to do the refreshing. Often relaxation is impossible until one has resigned oneself to living with one's difficulty, or until he has lost his personal turmoil in cosmic perspective.

Relaxation is a lesson important for the individual to learn especially in his late 20's and early 30's. At this time he is likely to discover the gap that exists between his initial aspirations and his abilities. A youth tends to have exaggerated expectations, and only later discovers that he is less clever than he thought, that he has to be satisfied with less income, less popularity, a less ideal marriage than he had hoped for. The discovery often leads to resentment, projection of blame, and profound distress and maladjustment. Relaxation and a cosmic perspective are very much needed to prepare for strong mental health in middle and later life.

Among the conditions especially subject to the law of reversed effect are the neurotic compulsions. A neurotic may know that he does the wrong and injurious thing but cannot help himself, and the more effort he expends on self-correction the worse matters become. His wrongdoing may, and often does, arouse acute feelings of guilt. If he is personally religious, he feels that his compulsions constitute an intolerable load of sin. Yet how can the neurotic sufferer, whose conduct is involuntary and whose impulses are prompted by mental tangles the nature of which is largely unknown to him, be held accountable for conduct that he consciously deplores? If freedom is a matter of choices available and known, does the neurotic have true freedom? If not, shall we dismiss his sense of sin as an infantile irrelevancy worthy of no respect?

Modern religion, I believe, would agree with the psychotherapist's position in this matter; but it would have one word to add. Any neurotic is living a life which in some respects is extreme in its self-centeredness. Even though many of his individual sentiments may be altruistic, the region of his misery represents a complete preoccupation with himself. The very nature of the neurotic disorder is tied to pride. If the sufferer is hypersensitive, resentful, captious, he may be indicating a fear that he will not appear to advantage in competitive situations where he wants to show his worth. If he is chronically indecisive, he is showing fear that he may do the wrong thing and be discredited. If he is over-scrupulous and self-critical, he may be endeavoring to show how praiseworthy he really is. Thus, though involuntary, partially unconscious, and uncontrollable in any direct way, most neuroses are, from the point of view of religion, mixed with the sin of pride. A more becoming basic humility, held in the religious perspective, could not help but improve the state of the sufferer's conscience, and thus indirectly affect favorably his mental health. Even when his compulsions get the better of him he need no longer regard them as of central importance in his life. As the focus of striving shifts from the conflict to selfless goals, the life as a whole becomes sounder even though the neurosis may never completely disappear.

Integration, for the neurotic or for the normal person, requires self-objectification. That is to say, it requires insight, a knowledge of one's values, a clear picture of one's assets and liabilities. Psychotherapy and religion agree on this point. Historically the church has had one very special aid for the inducing of self-objectification—the Confessional, or Sacrament of Penance. Some writers maintain that the traditional wisdom of religion in handling conflict by this means has been completely outstripped by the knowledge of the psychiatrist, who handles repression, dividedness of mind, guilt, better than does the religious method which may merely increase the conflict. Yet we know that some form of housecleaning is therapeutic, and that the relaxation and receptivity that accompany prayer may result in a new direction of healthful integrative thought. Some writers argue that it would now be well for psychiatry and consulting psychology to include more widely a revised form of confessional catharsis in their procedures.[10] One can confess to anyone, they say. Belief in absolution is not necessary.

William James, likewise enthusiastic about the confessional, and perplexed by its decline, writes:

For him who confesses, shams are over and realities have begun: he has exteriorized his rottenness. If he has not actually got rid of it, he at least no longer smears it over with a hypocritical show of virtue—he lives at least on a basis of veracity. The complete decay of the practice of confession in Anglo-Saxon communities is a little hard to account for.

Puzzling as to why Protestants gave up the practice of sacramental confession, he concludes:

We English-speaking Protestants, in the general self-reliance and unsociability of our nature, seem to find it enough if we take God alone into our confidence.[11]

There are, of course, important differences between secular and religious confession. In the latter, stress is laid exclusively upon one's own shortcomings. The shortcomings of others may not be discussed as, of course, they can be during a psychiatric interview. One is permitted to tell only one's own sins. This limitation prevents projections, shifting of blame, and uncharitable accusations. The believer who accepts the Sacrament of Penance feels that the past has been canceled, and that no debts carry over to the next page of life. He

---

[10] J. H. Leuba. *God or Man?* New York: Henry Holt, 1933, p. 316. Pierre Janet, especially interested in obsessive states, writes, "Regular confession seems to have been invented by a genius of an alienist who wanted to treat obsessions." *Les obsessions et la psychasténie*, Paris: F. Alcan, 1903, Vol. I, p. 707.

[11] W. James. *Op. cit.*, pp. 452 ff. Quoted by permission of Longmans, Green & Company.

accepts the priestly assurance that he may depart in peace. For the believer the authority involved is much greater than that wielded by any psychotherapist.

From the point of view of psychotherapy there is in this procedure one serious limitation. It provides no opportunity for exploring the environmental or interpersonal factors concerned in the conflict. The confessor is forbidden to approach the penitent outside the confessional for any further discussion of the problems raised. There is no opportunity for supplementary therapy, or for a full discussion of those aspects of the problem which in fact are due to the aggressions and transgressions of others. Priests, recognizing this limitation, have complained that parishioners do not come informally before or after confession for such auxiliary consultation as they need and as the priest is trained to supply.

Combining of Resources

In conclusion, I venture to restate three important facts. (1) The mental health of contemporary society is not good. Each year a larger segment of the population crosses the vague boundary-line that separates the region of normality from the dark territory beyond. Even among those who dwell securely in the land of normality, there is an excessive amount of avoidable anxiety, unhappiness, and confusion of purpose and thought. (2) The crux of mental health, and of much physical health, is found in the nature of the individual's beliefs: his minor beliefs about domestic and social situations in his immediate world, and major beliefs about the nature of the universe in which he lives. (3) It turns out that in many respects psychological science and religion, for all their differences in vocabulary, have similar views regarding the origin, nature, and cure for mental distress. Where emphasis and techniques differ, the relationship between psychotherapy and religion can often be regarded as one of desirable supplementation.

Although different kinds of people, according to the state of their own conscience, sentiments, and present wants, respond variously to different therapeutic opportunities, it is probable that for adequate coverage of the social need, at least three basic forms of service are required.

The first is the type of service offered by psychologists. A young and growing profession, consulting or clinical psychology aims to assist the individual in self-examination, self-assessment, and self-integration. Occasionally mental tests or vocational guidance are beneficial; often more significant is the value that comes from what today is called "nondirective therapy." It has been discovered that under appropriate circumstances the individual, facing a permissive, noncensorious listener, with a will to explore his life situation candidly, can, in the course of comparatively few hours, review and place in order his own values, consult his conscience, estimate his assets and liabilities, size up his conflicts, and often discover a course of conduct and thought that integrates his life far better than he considered possible without this simple therapeutic assistance.[12]

In principle, there is no reason why clergymen, trained in its use, or qualified individuals attached to churches, should not employ this first and simplest grade of therapy. But chiefly the clergy has the ability and obligation to supply the second type of service: offering spiritual advice and rules of life, or opportunities for religious confession when these are sought. Discussion and clarification of theological issues are wanted by some individuals. Others find in the church a needed social anchorage which provides a type of group

[12] Cf. C. R. Rogers. *Counseling and Psychotherapy*, Boston: Houghton Mifflin, 1942.

therapy. Group activities, we know, often stimulate a wholesome integration of thought and conduct, particularly in individuals who previously have felt isolated from their fellows. Even the somewhat disparaged technique of exhortation may have a place, for the wish to change one's behavior is the most potent single factor in one's capacity to change it. Where values are withered, or where the more socially desirable and inclusive values require reinforcement, exhortation at the right moment may prove efficacious.

Finally, there is psychiatric aid which for certain individuals is indispensable. Sedation, shock, depth analysis, may be the critical service to be rendered. It goes without saying that such forms of psychotherapy should not be engaged in excepting by well-trained psychiatrists.

If these three professional roads are pursued in a spirit of rivalry and isolation, the cause of mental health will be hindered. In certain instances separatism may seriously endanger the individual who, needing one type of service, falls only into the hands of a rival specialist. Fortunately in recent years we have witnessed the beginnings of coordination and cooperation in a common cause. These hopeful beginnings, I predict, will be greatly extended in the years that lie immediately ahead.

FIVE

The Nature of Doubt

THE PRIMARY THEME in the history of the world, Goethe has said, is the conflict between belief and unbelief. In certain epochs faith in some form reigns supreme. In others doubt gains the upper hand. Our own age, we know, is a period of doubt and negation.

This historical generalization can scarcely be questioned. Yet from the psychological point of view such a broad statement may imply too much. It may suggest that most mortals alive today are passively watching the ebbing tide of faith and waiting for some nameless catastrophe to wipe this doubting epoch from the slate of history. The psychological fact of the matter is that the conflict between belief and disbelief is a common enough condition of mind in any epoch. The frequency of the conflict may be greater at one time than another, but at bottom the conflict is individual in its form and in its functioning, as varied in flavor and significance as is personality itself.

The nature of belief will concern us in the next chapter. Here I wish to point out only that belief is the assent or affirmation that we feel respecting the existence of the object of a sentiment. Positive sentiments of any sort inevitably entail some grade of belief, and such belief always has motor concomitants, for what we believe we tend to act on. Negative sentiments likewise usually involve a belief in the existence of their rejected objects, although there are exceptions to this rule, as in the case of the atheist who both disbelieves in the deity and rejects the concept.

Besides the belief that is associated with sentiments there is also a kind of primitive credulity about things, most evident in the young child who believes almost anything he is told. Having learned to trust the first words he hears, to him all words that he understands are, for a while at least, as good as facts. Were he to hear that the moon is made of cheese, that God is a bear or a bearded man, he would be temporarily satisfied, and believe what he is told. The child's mind is thus furnished with many special beliefs before he discovers the important truth that words and facts are not identical. Among adults the same tendency to "verbal realism" is met, though in a reduced degree and only in regions where experience is limited, or where the prestige of the speaker arouses almost hypnotic deference. Verbal realism, we may say, is effective whenever interest is attended by only slight experience or by marked suggestibility toward the speaker. These conditions are especially marked in childhood, so much so that we may conclude that belief, based on primitive credulity, is prior to disbelief or doubt.

Disbelief is a negative, rejecting response or attitude. It comes normally after experience has counteracted the initial impulse to believe what has been presented to the senses or in words.

Doubt, like disbelief, is technically a secondary condition of mental life. It is an unstable or hesitant reaction, produced by the collision of evidence with prior belief, or of one belief with another. It is apparent that disbelief is relatively more final and single-minded than is doubt. Yet since doubt represents incipient disbelief, and since it springs from the same psychological sources, we shall be justified in treating these two states of mind together. For convenience we shall direct our remarks to the topic of *doubt*.

Although primitive credulity is primary and doubt secondary, the former readily gives way to the latter. Even in early childhood, beliefs are barely formed before they are put to test. It makes no difference whether, from the adult's point of view, the initial belief and the reasons for doubting are both unrealistic; to the child a dilemma and conflict exist. One child of three was perplexed by a problem he phrased as follows: "If I had gone upstairs, could God make it that I hadn't?" This child was already commencing to sense a clash between the alleged attributes of God's omnipotence and the hard reality of physical events. Such early stirrings of doubt are present some years before they result in sustained misgivings. It is frequently in the pre-puberty period that fatal collisions occur, when pennies have not fallen from heaven in response to a self-centered prayer, or when miracles are denied at a time when they would prove convenient, or when theological ideas have in some other way been tested to their disadvantage by developing experience. The lurid imagery of old-time theology and some of the more extravagant Bible stories inevitably pave the way for such misgivings. Only a child who is assisted in revising his imagery and his theology to accommodate the day-by-day increase in experience could escape the surge of doubt. Conceivably the parent and the church school might do a better job than they do in assisting the child over the successive collisions of belief and experience, and in helping him identify religion with a positive attitude toward life rather than with immature images and interests. Yet I question whether an outsider can detect the precise time when newly discovered fact is felt to clash with previously accepted belief. One trouble is that the parent cannot tell just what belief the child is harboring, for it almost certainly will be a juvenile distortion of what the parent has attempted to teach. Hence the integration of experience with sentiment can in only small part be met by the timely intervention of adults. Throughout the whole of life this integration is a personal quest. Even the wisest of persons who may have a well-thought-out, thoroughly mature solution, cannot pass it on like a well-wrapped package to another. Predicaments, experience, and aspirations are too individual in character to be fitted by a second-hand scheme of integration.

Nearly every moment of waking life seems to entail the trying out of various alternative potential beliefs. Is it going to rain this afternoon? Shall I trust this real estate agent or that? It has been rightly said that thinking is largely a matter of "vicarious trial and error," that is to say, of successive doubts and affirmations. Unless the individual doubts he cannot use his full intelligence, and unless he uses his full intelligence he cannot develop a mature sentiment.

Now it is characteristic of doubt that it assails most strongly the higher levels of interpretation. We have a ready enough acceptance of what we call facts, and a high degree of social agreement concerning them, for the simple reason that we define a fact as that which is verifiable by commonly acceptable tests. But facts, thus defined, are specific objects or happenings. When we come to explain them or to evaluate them, or tell their larger significance, our paths of interpretation diverge. Facts never speak for themselves. Every biological fact, for example, can be fitted into at least two broadly inclusive hypotheses—a mechanistic and a vitalistic. In psychology, there are many schools of thought distinguished by their characteristic preference for one or another style of interpreting the facts that are common to all schools. So far as natural science is concerned, the higher levels of interpretation, dealing with issues of probability, causation, reality, slip into the field of philosophy where plural hypotheses abound. Religion, aiming to deal with the most inclusive of relationships—aiming to bind fact, value, and ultimate reality—is the most controversial, the most doubt-ridden, the most elusive of all the fields of mental activity. It would be so, even if the temper of the times did not at present intensify the situation. Having turned from religion to higher education, great masses of people regard the former as an obscurantism from which they must emerge. They have learned the first lesson taught by higher education which is to avoid being duped. The first lesson is all that many ever learn.

It is not the function of the psychologist to pass on the legitimacy or illegitimacy of any doubt. His duty is merely to elucidate a process which he finds to be a universal and necessary part of mental life. He holds that if each person understood the doubting process, he would be in a better position to determine the cogency of his own grounds for belief or disbelief. Although each individual has his own history, pattern, and degree of misgiving, there are certain modes of doubt that seem especially common. The modes that I shall distinguish are, I think, those most often encountered. It goes without saying that any single individual may entertain several of these styles of doubting.

Doubts Primarily Reactive and Negativistic

First, the ardor that lies behind militant atheism needs to be examined. It was said of one zealous apostle of free-thought that he believed in No-God and worshiped Him; of another, that he would believe anything, so long as it was not in the Bible. Such acute negativism is "emotionally over-determined." In some instances we can trace a history of trauma, as in the case of the soldier who in the very act of praying was blinded and crippled by a shell that burst near by. Other lives, too, have known tragedies too shattering to be incorporated into such a religious sentiment as they may previously have had. A violent shock can change a positive attitude into a negative.

In other cases of reactivity the unconscious mental life seems decisive. If, as Freud has said, the religious sentiment is at bottom an extension of one's attitude toward one's physical father, then we must expect repressed animosity toward this father on occasion to be reflected in a hatred of religion. It seems curious that while Freud insists that belief in God is a projection of dependence and love associated with the earthly father, he overlooks the fact that by the same token atheism may be construed as the projection of ambivalence or hatred associated with the male parent. Probably the truest statement would be that on occasion—probably not often—both belief and doubt may reflect unconsciously one's attitudes toward one's parent.

The subtle relation between militant atheism and positive religion has sometimes been pointed out. "Atheism, rightly understood," writes Spengler, "is the necessary expression of a spirituality that has exhausted its religious possibilities. . . . It is entirely compatible with a living wistful desire for real religiousness—therein resembling Romanticism, which likewise would recall that which has irrevocably gone."[1] By reacting so violently against religion, an ardent atheist in reality betrays a deep interest in the religious mode of life. "Reaction formation" is the term psychologists apply to people who disguise real interests with violent protests. Even those atheists who are not passionate or querulous sometimes betray themselves as fundamentally, though unconventionally, religious in their orientation toward life. Robert G. Ingersoll, regarded as an atheist in his time, wrote:

[1] Oswald Spengler. *Decline of the West*, New York: Alfred A. Knopf, translated 1926, p. 408. Quoted by permission.

I belong to the Great Church which holds the world within its starlit aisles; that claims the great and good of every race and clime; that finds with joy the grain of gold in every creed, and floods with light and love the germs of good in every soul.[2]

Such discourse, if liberal, is certainly religious. Thus atheism is not always the antithesis of religion, especially if it betrays deep interest in the goings-on of religion. People are often called atheists, and often call themselves so, for no other reason than that they do not believe in a generally approved definition of God.

One of the commonest states of mind at the present time is "religious agnosticism" wherein individuals react against formal religion lest it impede the free exercise of their minds, but at the same time often maintain the highest standards of ethical conduct, and may vaguely relate these standards to the moments of reverence and wonder that they occasionally experience. The point to note is that in reacting against the intellectual slavery of an idea, the resulting negativism often pertains to specific content rather than to basic values.

Reactive doubters are, of course, genuine doubters, and the origins of their misgivings have nothing to do with the legitimacy or illegitimacy of their disbelief. But it is well to bear in mind that not a few so-called atheists, and many agnostics, humanists, and anti-clericists, at bottom show a suspiciously deep concern about the whole subject.

Doubts Associated with Violations of Self-interest

We need not linger on the second mode of doubting which springs from violations of self-interest, for I have called attention to it on several occasions. The initial egocentric phase of

[2] R. G. Ingersoll. Declaration, *North American Review*, 1888, 146, p. 46.

religious development, as we have seen, is marked by a kind of primitive grossness. The child who finds his personal advantage not immediately and satisfactorily served by his prayers may discard his conceptions and terminate once and for all his religious quest. Sometimes the issue comes to a head only later in life, in conjunction with acute personal need. "Prayer does not stop bullets," was the refrain of many veterans; "they perforate both devout and infidel." "Religion has no survival value for me." A faith centered in self-advantage is bound to break up. To endure at all it must envisage a universe that extends beyond personal whim and is anchored in values that transcend the immediate interest of the individual as interpreted by himself.

The Shortcomings of Organized Religion

Common in these days, and especially among younger people, is the doubt engendered by visible hypocrisy and failure in institutional religion. Some select out doctrines or practices that seem repressive to intelligence. They see in religion only a set of scruples designed to limit the free exercise of thought. One soldier found himself revolted during his visit to Jerusalem by the commercialization of the stations of the cross where postcard sellers and souvenir vendors clamored greedily, and by the fees charged for the blessing of rosaries purchased in the Church of the Holy Sepulchre. Vulgarity, exploitation, money-changing, in the Christian church after twenty centuries of existence seemed inexcusable. Tracing backward the history of organized religion, other doubters shudder at the record of cruelty, oppression, deceit, at the burning of heretics, the torture of Jews, the hounding of Mormons, the persecution of Catholics, the massacre of infidels. Have the great world religions, the doubter asks, really progressed beyond the tribal creeds that encouraged groveling superstition, xenophobia, cannibalism, headhunting?

To one who fixes attention upon this history of horror, the excesses committed in the name of religion, perhaps because of the sheer intensity of feeling released, seem to exceed the evil of which disbelievers are capable. Within the fold of organized religion bigots and brutes exist, while outside the fold are many considerate, selfless men.[3] If the adherents of institutional religion and its leaders do not pass the test why should one not doubt the validity of the way of life they profess to follow?

This mode of doubting is widespread especially among youth who today seem supersensitive to the darker spots of religious history. Nor are doubters persuaded by the counter-argument that crimes of persecution and bigotry are to be charged up to secularism and corruption rather than to the religious hypothesis in its purity.

God in Man's Image

Humanists are particularly disturbed at the discovery that the God-concept changes according to the condition of man. Viewing the history of religion in perspective one notes how in the beginning there were a multiplicity of deities. Monotheism came later. Originally the gods were limited in nature and capricious in conduct. Jehovah, by contrast, was supreme and steadfast. The first gods had to do primarily with nature, but then came a God of persons who prized individuality. Earlier deities, indifferent to man, were throned afar, but were displaced by an indwelling God of profound moral concern. As man became increasingly aware of himself, God was seen as coming closer to man.[4] The relation of such relativism to disbelief is plain enough.

[3] The malfeasances of organized religion are listed with enthusiasm by J. H. Leuba. *God or Man?* New York: Henry Holt, 1933, Chapters 17 and 18.

[4] Cf. Max Schoen. *Thinking about Religion*, New York: Philosophical Library, 1946, p. 42.

To say that there is a God is not to say anything more than that we need to think that there is, and the need is in no sense a guarantee of the existence of that which satisfied it. Thus the great religions of the world are not theology, but psychology; witnesses, not to the attributes of God, but to the inventive faculty of man. God is not a real being; He is the image of man, projected, enlarged, upon the empty canvas of the universe.[5]

That man's inventive faculty enters into his religious ideas is a fact no psychologist can question. Projection is one of our commonest and slyest mental tricks, especially when certainty of knowledge is lacking. Whether the existence of projection in religious thinking invalidates the hypothesis that God exists is a question that will be settled in different ways by different people. The humanist will conclude that the projection of human fantasy upon divine "objects" proves that the latter are illusory. The religious person will say that our halting and fanciful efforts to grasp the nature of the deity do not invalidate His existence. The Gospel of India, the *Bhagavad Gita*, expresses this latter view:

> Some see me one with themselves, or separate:
> Some bow to the countless gods that are only
> My million faces.[6]

Doubts Associated with the Genesis of the Religious Quest

We come now to a related mode of doubting that is of special interest to the psychologist. It takes its start from the facts reviewed in our first lecture. Religious strivings, we there learned, often originate in the desires of the body, in the pursuit of meanings beyond the range of our intellectual

[5] C. E. M. Joad. *The Present and Future of Religion*, London: Ernest Benn Ltd., 1930, p. 108. Quoted by permission.

[6] Translated by Swami Prabhavananda and Christopher Isherwood. Hollywood: Marcel Rodd Co., 1944, p. 105.

capacity, and in the longing that values be conserved. Do we not then merely "rationalize" our yearnings with manufactured beliefs that are egomorphic, fashioned to satisfy private desire or inner compulsion? Does not the very prominence of the fear motive indicate that we have invented a God to protect us against anxiety? And if life or society demands many renunciations from us, are we not prone to invent an after-life that will compensate us for present deprivation?

This mode of doubting is especially common in our psychological era. No enlightened person wishes to be duped by his desires, his fantasies, his glands. The presence of transparent self-deceptions in everyday life, and in much self-centered religion, puts one on guard against the perils of wishful thinking and cheap rationalizing. Anyone who has learned about this matter (and who, by now, has not?) grows suspicious of beliefs that owe their origin to frustration, to fear, to temperament, and to cultural suggestion.

Since the psychologist is responsible for introducing the protean concept of rationalization—or rather for changing its meaning from the search for true and adequate reason to the search for specious justificatory reason—it is up to the psychologist to issue certain warnings. In reversing the original meaning of rationalization he has inadvertently suggested that there is no such thing as bona fide reason. He has implied that every belief is a product of irrational forces. "Once one has grasped the meaning of rationalization, its use in controversy is fascinatingly easy. You need not examine your opponent's arguments at all. You need only state what you imagine to be the affective grounds of his opinions, and dismiss all his reasons as rationalizations."[7]

Unless employed with great circumspection, the charge

---

[7] R. H. Thouless. *An Introduction to the Psychology of Religion*, Cambridge, England: University Press, 1928, p. 84. Quoted by permission.

"you are rationalizing" becomes a boomerang. In our discussion of atheism, for example, we saw that there is often an emotionally determined need to disprove the existence of God. Hence if the atheist says to the believer, "You only believe in God because you find some personal satisfaction in so doing," the believer can retort with equal justification, "And how about yourself?" A reckless young student, who had a smattering of psychology, once attacked Archbishop Temple with the accusation, "You only believe what you believe because of your early upbringing." The Archbishop promptly dispatched him with the reply, "You only believe that I believe what I believe because of my early upbringing, because of *your* early upbringing." Thus the boomerang returns. If one's background may be said to be the reason for belief, it may also be said to be the reason for disbelief. And the argument has progressed not at all.

The plain truth is that origins can tell nothing about the validity of a belief. Neither can origins characterize the mature belief as it now exists, nor explain its part in the present economy of a life. One of the best musicians I know took up his profession originally, in part at least, because he was taunted in childhood for what seemed to be his tone-deafness. In psychological parlance, he "overcompensated" for the defect. But that incident has absolutely nothing to do with the present structure or dynamics of his life-absorbing interest. We spoke in an earlier chapter of the fact that, when well-formed, the mature religious sentiment develops a driving power in its own right, motivating action, transforming character, and ordering sub-systems of belief and conduct. This view, ascribing functional autonomy to the operation of the religious sentiment, is the precise opposite of the view which mistakenly holds that the infantile roots of a sentiment for all time provide the forces for sustaining the sentiment and measuring its worth.

Were we to gauge our evaluations by origin we would disparage the eloquence of Demosthenes because his oratory served as a compensation for his tendency to stammer. We would depreciate Schumann's music because it may have been touched by his psychosis. The rationalism of Kant's philosophy would be invalid because it represented at the outset his protest against the hypochondria induced by his sunken chest. Longfellow's benignant outlook on life would be discredited since it served to rationalize his comfortable Victorian existence. Quakerism with its inner voice of guidance would be worthless because the founder of Quakerism, George Fox, suffered severe hallucinations. St. Paul's vision on the road to Damascus would have no significance because it may have been epileptoid in character. And the fact that many psychologists take up their science because of personal maladjustments would make psychology worthless.

The mistaken view that higher mental operations, originating in personal motivation, are therefore rationalizations and untrustworthy is called by logicians the "genetic fallacy." Unlike other modes of doubting it is basically illegitimate, and cannot be permitted a part in any discussion of religion.

Scientific Doubting

We come now to a more impressive mode of doubting, one that arises out of the scientist's professional habits of thought. Doubting is one of his specialties, and as likely as not it affects his outlook on religion. Nowadays if you ask concerning a person, "What is his religion?" the reply may well be, "Why, he hasn't any religion; he's an intellectual." Although the majority of people are not scientists or intellectuals, so great is the prestige of science and so rapidly is its influence spreading through universal education, that scientific habits of thought are gradually extending themselves throughout the population as a whole.

To debate the issue of science and religion is not within our scope; but to clarify the psychological reasons for their characteristic differences in modes of thinking is part of our task. Scientific doubters, no less than religious believers, are simply human individuals who have evolved in their course of living certain guiding sentiments for their thinking, what Fromm calls "frames of orientation and devotion."

The scientific mode of thought is marked by deeply ingrained habits, congruent with deeply ingrained sentiments. Foremost among these is the limitation of interest imposed by the scientist's routine. Hour after hour, day after day, his attention is held to limited and accessible segments of nature —perhaps the tensile strength of steel, the learning ability of the child, or the properties of the carbon ring. His rewards come from his detailed discoveries, from riveting himself to the microcosm, and by excluding the macrocosm. Accustomed, within his microcosm, to say, "I don't know," he finds it easy to confront the macrocosm with doubt. So exacting are the demands of his day that in leisure hours he is unlikely to turn to the intellectual puzzles of the macrocosm, but prefers to turn to fishing, to art, to friends, to family.

Not only is the scientist's curiosity limited by his professional habits, but he has come to rely upon a small range of acceptable techniques for discovering truth. One of his technical requirements is that any working hypothesis he uses must be closely relevant to the task in hand. So remote an hypothesis as the existence of God is not particularly helpful in tracing the properties of carbon rings or of learning curves. In the past a limiting conception of the deity has been a hindrance to free scientific inquiry. Another technical requirement is that the investigator keep himself out of his work. Should he care too much for his hypothesis his objectivity will fail. The intrusion of personal interest into science is felt to spell disaster. Recognizing that religion minus the personal factor is nothing at all, the scientist sees it as a violation of ingrained habit and finds it distasteful.

Yet another habit asserts itself. The scientist does not accept statements unless they can be verified by individuals employing acceptable operations. Although St. Theresa was certain she had seen the Trinity, her testimony is inadmissible regarding the existence of the Trinity. Not all of the mystics of all the ages taken together can prove that their sense of God is a grauantee of God's existence. It is easily understandable from the naturalistic point of view why human beings should have faith, for the religious urge reflects "a primitive tendency, possessing biological survival value, to unify our environment so that we can cope with it." The religious sentiment is thus merely the "culmination of a basic tendency or organisms to react in a configurational way to situations."[8] But in itself the configurational urge is a guarantee of nothing objective.

As a disciplined, intelligent, hardworking individual, the scientist is likely to be an ethical person. Seeing morality in himself, he concludes that religion is not indispensable to good living in the social sense. He has his own social creed, believing that peace and prosperity will stem from education, higher living standards, full employment, and rational social organization. With such improvements man can scarcely ask for more salvation. If the scientist is reminded that his ethical aims are derived from the Hebrew-Christian tradition,

[8] H. Hoagland. Some comments on science and faith, in *Science, Philosophy and Religion: a Symposium*, New York: Conference on Science, Philosophy, Religion, 1941, Chapter 3, p. 36. This chapter, from which I have drawn several of my points, is an excellent statement of the case for religious agnosticism.

he replies that in the future, he thinks, empirical sanctions, drawn somehow from science, will be sufficient to dictate the good life without further recourse to supernatural sanctions. Reminded that up to now scientific techniques have yielded nothing that would enable men to distinguish between values and disvalues, he may shrug and reply, "I never expect to understand most of the things that I value most highly—the thrill of a sunset, of a symphony, or the love I have for certain persons. But I prefer to admit my failure to understand rather than to accept explanations based on a type of evidence I cannot accept as valid."[9]

The scientist's habits or thought have proven to be brilliantly productive; so much so that any system of faith that does not maintain complete adaptability toward the discoveries of science, finds itself now, and will find itself henceforth, on the defensive. Yet to the mature religious thinker the scientific frame of thought, though thoroughly honest, seems limited. Every person, he points out, is compelled to build his life on probabilities that are far less certain than those of science. Moral and political commitments, the affirmation of this purpose or that, the superiority of love over hate, rest ultimately on no scientific ground. From the point of view of the religious frame, the scientist seems to be living a sparse existence, unable to coordinate his professional thoughts with the rest of his life. His limiting habits, exercised through long use, have cramped his sensitivities. Darwin, at the age of sixty, complained that he could no more enjoy Shakespeare, for he had too long disciplined his mind to conceive reality as limited, verifiable, one-faceted. Integration of personality, thinks the religionist, is hindered if scientific discipline dominates the life. This accusation is interesting, for to the scientist the shoe seems to be on the other foot. To him those who maintain religious beliefs are said to do

[9] *Ibid.*, p. 38.

so only by virtue of keeping their faith in one compartment and their science in another. It is *their* mental integrity that suffers. But the religionist is still insistent, arguing that his search is far more comprehensive in its scope than is the scientist's, and that the scientific agnostic cannot but lack a sense of the continuity of the universe. Is it always true, as the scientist insists, that observation and understanding are necessarily more accurate when they are unemotional and impersonal? Is one not better able to perceive congruence in the universe as a whole when one is reverently receptive? Emotion may be an aid and not merely a hindrance to discovery. To stand wholly outside the phenomenon is to understand it less well than by entering in.

The fact that values are not included within the scientific frame of thought is at the present moment causing widespread consternation. The productions of natural science, notably the release of atomic energy, have made everyone, including scientists, aware that the utilization of these productions, without the application of prior moral principles, can lead to disaster. The fact that the truths of science are devalued turns out to be a peril. Scientists themselves, as has been pointed out, are ordinarily well-intentioned men, but their good intentions seem closeted from their technical activity. Were they to bring together into an embracing system the facts they discover and the values they hold, would they not be forced to construct a single, more comprehensive frame of reference, one that would verge toward the religious?

Finally, to many religious minds it seems their own habits of thought and those of the scientist, in spite of their differences, have one similarity. Each type of mind engenders hypotheses which must be tested by living. If not adequately verified, the hypothesis should be discarded. The difference here lies in the fact that any system of religious faith has much more to test. The hypotheses of science are ordinarily confirmed by the successful predicting of limited happenings, while faith must locate the whole gamut of concrete happenings within a moral, aesthetic, and cosmological order. It must assign a prominent place to the personal factor which science seeks to exclude, and top it all with a congruent theology. The pyramid is higher; the strain is greater; the tests applied will inevitably be less rigorous and markedly different in type. By comparison, the verifications of the scientist are clean and easy. He chooses certainty in preference to adequacy. Religion can never pretend to rest its case on certainty, but only on the legitimacy of its effort to find reasonable certitude within the domain of adequacy.

Not only do the habits of thought, the expectations and demands, appropriate to the scientific and to the religious frame differ markedly, but at any given moment of time, they seem irreconcilable. The axioms on which a scientist proceeds while he is acting scientifically are at odds with axioms on which a person proceeds when he is acting religiously. By axiom we mean some fundamental proposition that is admitted without debate in order to give form and fluency to a course of thought that is under way. Although no human mind can entertain contrary axioms at one and the same moment of time, alternation between axioms is very common. On a winter evening we take out the checkerboard. Shall we play checkers or give-away? The axioms in the two games are different. Or we take out the playing cards. Shall we have our poker straight or with deuces wild? One set of axioms or the other must be accepted. We travel from the United States to England, and shift our monetary and traffic axioms accordingly. Clearly we are accustomed to keeping our axioms in logic-tight compartments.[10]

---

[10] The case for this dualism is well presented by H. M. Johnson, Can religion blend with modern science? *The Virginia Quarterly Review*, 1930, 6, 321–334.

In playing the game of science, a definite set of axioms must be adopted. They include, first and foremost, the principle of determinism. Identical happenings, with identical histories, will have identical futures. There can be no intervention of Providence. Although laws may be beyond our present capacity to unravel, still the axiom of determinism must always be held; otherwise the game of science, as now conceived, cannot be played.

Yet the axiom of determinism, indispensable to the maintenance of the scientific frame of thought, has never been proved in any absolute sense. While in the laboratory the axiom is fruitful, outside, the scientist customarily rejects it. He proceeds, for example, on the assumption that he and his fellow men have freedom of choice respecting their conduct. He praises and blames, admonishes and exhorts, judges and punishes, consults his conscience and puts forth effort— none of these activities consistent with the axiom of determinism.

How is it with the axiom that private worlds of experience are inadmissible as scientific evidence? A necessary axiom for the scientist in the laboratory, it is a bad axiom for him outside. For it turns out that the acceptable tests of love and beauty, happiness and pain, of every single value by which he lives, are the revelation of direct experience alone.

And so we see that no single set of axioms, not even the scientific set, can be maintained consistently at all levels of existence. What then happens in the clash between scientific and religious axioms? Each person handles the clash in his own way, usually as a version of one of three logical possibilities.

First, scientific disbelief may emerge triumphant, because the axioms of science are on the whole preferred. Owing to sentiment and habit they constitute what William James would call a "livelier option." If their insufficiency for present living is recognized, they are nonetheless declared to be in principle on the right track, and contrary considerations can for the time being be disregarded.

Secondly, the individual with a more flexible sentiment structure may decide that while religious axioms and scientific axioms cannot blend, there is something to be said for each. At one time he gladly accepts the axiom of determinism, at another the axiom of freedom. He admits the validity of direct knowledge on some occasions, not on others. Thus a frank dualism, perhaps even two master-sentiments, mark the life, which he justifies on the indisputable basis that every person does inevitably in the course of living accept contradictory axioms according to circumstance.[11]

The third possibility is a ceaseless struggle to assimilate the scientific frame of thought within an expanded religious frame. A person with a mature religious sentiment characteristically attempts this course, and though he seldom succeeds perfectly, he continues to affirm the ultimate possibility of so doing. Under no circumstances will he side-step or disparage the scientific mode of doubting, but under no circumstances will he allow it to curtail the range of his curiosity or aspiration.

Before leaving our comparison of the two frames of thought, I venture a final observation. In one important respect the conflict between science and religion is less acute today than in former decades. Modern society emerged from a state of complete theological domination. Progress almost inevitably meant that scientific discoveries contradicted earlier religious lore. But nowadays, to put the matter baldly, youth learns science first. Instead of perceiving evolution, nuclear physics, and psychoanalysis against the grounds of the older theology, he learns first that man is part of the organic universe, within the biological realm a member of the animal

[11] Cf. H. M. Johnson, *loc. cit.*

species, and socialized through learning processes. Then he
wonders whether this account is adequate. How about man's
imagination, purpose, idealism, values? How about a first
cause? In this course of development, religion may take a
more favored position than formerly. Instead of serving as the
stale ground from which scientific insights dazzlingly emerge,
religion may be perceived as the fresh and sparkling insight
needed to supplement and correct the lifeless and de-valued
ground of science.

Referential Doubting

I have left until last the commonest mode of doubting,
one that derives from science but today is widely linked to
common sense. It is the recurrent conflict between acceptable
standards of evidence and this or that specific content of
religious teaching. How, with twentieth-century enlighten-
ment, can one believe in traditional statements regarding the
fieriness of Hell, the golden pavements of Heaven, the pillar
of salt that was Lot's wife, the resurrection of the body,
miracles, and all the rest of it? This mode of doubting, it
will be noted, does not challenge the religious way of life
nor the religious treatment of values, but only those statements which, if taken literally, would offend the ordinary
canons of comprehension. To a modern mind, searching for
explicit referents, the sacred literature of all religions fares
badly. Scriptures written one, two, or three thousand years
ago are archaic and equivocal; their explanations of natural
phenomena have long been in full retreat. I venture to say
that there is no adherent of any religion, and perhaps never
has been, who has failed to find certain statements within
his accepted system of faith incomprehensible or dubious.
Contemporary semantics, which is in part a psychological

discipline, has something to say regarding this mode of doubting. Only a very small fraction of discourse, it tells us, is designative in its significance, pointing unequivocally to specific and tangible referents. When you and I pass on the street, our conversation may consist entirely of the exchange of phrases, "Nice day!" "Yes, isn't it?" Now we don't mean that it is a nice day, at least we don't mean only that. We are saying, "Well, here we are, crossing paths; I know who you are; you know who I am. I am not hostile to you; I assume you are not hostile to me. Let's get along now and be about our respective businesses." Such discourse is purely rhetorical, what is sometimes called "phatic." When Goethe wrote, "Green is life's golden tree," he did not mean that life's tree, whatever that may be, is either green or gold, certainly not both green and gold. He meant something, and something important, but his mode of discourse, instead of being designative, was appraisive and poetic. When Christ said, "Ye must be born again," the literal-minded Nicodemus was puzzled and asked, "Can a man enter a second time into his mother's womb and be born?" A statement intended to be prescriptive and incitive was mistaken for something informative and designative. Of sixteen modes of discourse listed by Morris, one only is informative-designative, that is to say *scientific* in its referential character. "Around every religion," says Morris, "there grows in time a body of critical discourse (a theology) which aims to defend systematically the way of life approved by the religion." Now its adequacy depends entirely upon whether this discourse succeeds in representing somehow the total orientation of the personality, providing a satisfactory focus and direction to the life as a whole.[12] Under no circumstances can the signification of religious discourse be judged by applying tests of literal meaning.

[12] Charles Morris. *Signs, Language and Behavior*, New York: Prentice-Hall, 1946, pp. 125, 147.

Yet in pondering the specific content of religious teaching most minds do hesitate between literal and figurative interpretations. The positivism of our times has made us particularly critical of statements that sound designative but are not. It urges us to relegate to the category of superstition all views of reality that do not square with verifiable sensory impression. In its contemporary form of operationism, positivism denies the possibility of speaking intelligibly at all about metaphysical ideas, moral assumptions, or supernatural concepts. Therefore, the entire realm of religion, being inaccessible to operational exploration, is meaningless. Such extremism in methodology, of course, condemns nearly all poetic, artistic, legal discourse along with the religious, and most other forms for human communication as well.

The difficulty arises from the fact that religion has to use many of the same signs as science does. Images based upon space and time seem about all that are available. The ascension is a literal rising up to heaven; the end of the world is a definite event in time; hell is downward; heaven a glittering corridor on high. It was William James who said that in religious thinking we make use of such poor symbols as our life affords. It is unfortunate that they must be the same symbols that do duty for common sense and for scientific discourse. Confusion, with consequent doubts, is bound to arise.

What shall we say about the Fundamentalist who prides himself on believing every word in the Bible? Can he mean what he says? The Bible affirms, "There is no God," but adds, "says the fool in his heart." Even the Fundamentalist must take the context into account. How about the parables? Christ himself meant them not to be taken literally but metaphorically. Relative to the Modernist, the Fundamentalist does cling so far as he can to concrete images, and takes Biblical discourse so far as he can as designative; but even he is far less literal-minded than he thinks.

The immense storehouse of religious symbols, in words, in paintings, in music, in ritualistic acts, is an accretion to which countless aspiring mortals have contributed. It is not to be expected that any one individual here and now will find all this symbolic accumulation congenial or intelligible. Inevitably there are statements in sacred writing and in tradition that seem meaningless, even repulsive. Yet what chills one seeker may warm another. Personalities are infinitely varied. It is for this reason that doubters who cavil at the unclarity or unacceptability of any particular symbol are speaking only for themselves. A re-forming of religious symbols to give greater designative fidelity for one person would merely throw others into a new state of doubt. A clergyman of my acquaintance takes pains to confess to his congregation that he does not believe in the resurrection of the body. One may admire his candor, yet caution him regarding the consequences of shifting religious discourse into the realm of scientific and designative discourse. Creeds, like rituals, mean much more than they seem to say.

I do not mean to imply that religious language has no representative function at all. Some statements regarding historical and theological fact are too definite to be circumvented by declaring them to mean whatever the individual wants them to mean. Various religious sects are in fact defined by a common set of symbols having approximately common significance for all members. Yet, the essential psychological situation remains: of all the modes of human discourse, the religious is inevitably the one that is used with the greatest latitude, and the one to which the demand for specifically agreed upon referents least applies. The reason is that the cosmic conditions pointed to in religious language are not demonstrable, not knowable (in their entirety), and therefore not accurately signifiable. Words, as Whitehead has said, were apparently invented for the purpose of making discriminations within the microcosm. As soon as they are applied to macroscopic conceptions they grow elusive. The more abstract a term the more various is the individual's definition of its meanings, and we have no terms more abstract than those employed by religion.

What religious language signifies primarily are aspiration, self-imposed ideals, approval of one way of life and disapproval of others. It signifies the hoped-for completion of knowledge and the intended perfection of one's own nature. Most people, accustomed to worship, know this fact well, and generally report that, as time goes on, the specific content of a religious service means less to them, while the service as a whole means more. A recent empirical study demonstrates this tendency in reference to prayer. It was found that with increase in religious practice there often goes increased preference for prayers containing beauty and dignity of expression and a corresponding loss of preference for prayers which contain approved single ideas or subject-matter. What grows is the *intent* of the whole act of worship, while the importance of specific *content* recedes.[13]

Many religious systems recognize this fact. Hindu worship enjoins the thousand-fold repetition of the believer's own private name for God, with a special intention to confer meaning upon what would otherwise be a repetitive and routine act. The Catholic Mass is said over and over with the intention to glorify God, and usually with some added special intention for each occasion. When religious intention is steadfast enough it may overlay, and in time overcome, misgivings associated with this or that troublesome item of content.

We conclude, therefore, that doubt less often arises from a consideration of the long-range intent of the religious sentiment than from preoccupation with the constituent images

[13] A. T. Welford. An attempt at an experimental approach to the psychology of religion, *British Journal of Psychology*, 1946, 36, 55–73.

and symbols that unavoidably accompany the expression of the sentiment. Doubters have a habit of fixing attention upon the content that assists our thoughts. But attention, as the poet George Herbert assures us, may be fixated far as well as near:

> He who looks on glass,
>   On it may stay his eye;
> Or if he pleaseth through it pass,
>   And then the heavens espy.

The Nature of Faith

IN THE PREVIOUS CHAPTER I stated that belief normally seems to develop in three stages. There is first a period of raw credulity, most clearly seen in the child who believes indiscriminately in the evidence of his senses, of his imagination, and in what he hears. His first religious beliefs are derived chiefly from what he hears, that is, from "verbal realism." To him words are as good as facts. That some of this primitive credulity lasts throughout life is evident, but chiefly, I think, in minds marked by arrested development, or in areas where we are starkly ignorant or in the face of strong prestige suggestion. Some religious belief among adults is of this unquestioning variety—childish, authoritarian, and irrational.

Normally, however, a second stage of development disrupts the first. Doubts of the many sorts we have considered flood into one's life. They are an integral part of all intelligent thinking. Until one has faced the improbabilities involved in any commitment one is not free to form an independent conviction based on productive thinking and observing.

Mature belief, the third stage, grows painfully out of the alternating doubts and affirmations that characterize productive thinking. We evolve our important beliefs *pari passu* with our values and our sentiments. When I say I believe in education, in civil rights, in the United Nations, I mean that these intangible objects are regarded by me not only as *existing* but also as *desirable* and wholly consonant with my personal sentiment-structure. They are necessary to me if I am to fulfill the course of development that has now become my essential style of life. All positive sentiments entail belief of this sort. For without belief one could not act in keeping with one's sentiments, and if one could not act out one's sentiments one soon would lose them. It is important to remark that beliefs may be held with all grades of certainty. Even a relatively unsure belief can marshal a great deal of energy. One does not know for certain that the United Nations can save civilization from collapse, but one can be loyal and helpful if one at least believes there is a good chance.

Is "faith" the same as "belief"? Often the words are used interchangeably, although more often there is a difference in connotation. We tend to speak of faith when we are designating the less sure beliefs. We believe our eyes, and we believe the proposition that twice two are four, but we have faith in America, or in the ultimate triumph of good over evil. There is, of course, a borderline of discourse where we can use either term. "I believe in the United Nations" means much the same as "I have faith in the United Nations."

"Faith" also seems to carry a warmer glow of affection than does bare "belief." It suggests that though the risk may be greater, still the commitment is stronger and the outcome of the wager more precious. Most people, when asked, say they believe in God. But in many of these cases the reply seems perfunctory, and one suspects that the religious sentiment behind the statement is rudimentary. But when an individual says, "I have faith in God," it seems almost certain that the religious sentiment holds a prominent place in his personality-structure.

This excursion into semantics has no particular importance for our purpose excepting to indicate that faith is probably more complex psychologically than is simple belief. Although the term may be used in connection with any sentiment, it is most characteristically used in connection with the religious sentiment. And this fact seems to signify that we are dimly aware of the special intricacies involved in the affirmations arising from this sentiment.

The Religious Intention

The maturely productive religious sentiment, I have argued throughout these pages, is an interest-system within the structure of an individual's personality basically like any other well-developed interest-system. Like other mature sentiments it is *well differentiated*, which means that the individual at various times can view its sub-parts and their relation to one another; it is *dynamic* in its own right, that is, it plays an important autonomous part in the motivational life of the individual regardless of its own origins; it is *productive of conduct consistent with the nature of the sentiment*, and engenders a conscience appropriate to the values involved. Because of its special nature, however, the religious sentiment in some respects does differ in degree if not in kind from other mature sentiments. It is certainly more *comprehensive*, since it aims to join all experience into a single meaningful system. It is likewise a *uniquely integral system* in that it aims to give one leading directive to the life as a whole. Finally, because of the limited certainties that plague any religious belief, there is an *heuristic* quality to this sentiment: it is held with loyalty for the very purpose of discovering all the good and all the truth that may issue from it.

Now it seems to me that these distinctive features of the religious sentiment must lead us to expect a somewhat distinctive character in religious faith—as opposed to any other sort of faith. Specifically, I propose that we look for that peculiar character in mature religious faith that attends its comprehensiveness, its integral and its heuristic character.

The simplest way to start our search is to examine two profoundly religious utterances from Thomas à Kempis, *De Imitatione Christi*. The first is in the form of a supplication:

> Comfort my banishment;
> Assuage my sorrow;
> For my whole desire sigheth after Thee.

The phrase, "my whole desire sigheth after Thee," expresses with classic simplicity the attributes of comprehensiveness and integrality in the developed religious sentiment.

The second quotation is a brief homily:

If God were always the pure intention of our desire, we should not be so easily troubled.

Am I wrong in seeing in this passage a recognition of the heuristic character of religious faith? Is it not saying that if faith were adequate the believer would find his riddles solved and his anxieties allayed? He would make discoveries of knowledge and of value.

But the feature of this quotation of special importance to us is the author's use of *intention*. God, he says, may be "the pure intention of our desire." What does he mean? To explain this statement psychologically is not easy, for American psychology up to now has dealt very little with phenomenological concept of intention. Yet it is my opinion that little progress can be made in the understanding of the individual and his religion without the aid of precisely this concept.

The Meaning of Intention

The first modern psychologist to give intention a prominent place in his system of thought was Brentano, the Austrian.[1] For him the one fundamental characteristic of human life is the mental *act*. To act mentally is to *intend* an object that represents our goal. One can name no condition of mental life that is not one of stretching toward, aiming at, or otherwise intending a goal. Always the individual is *trying* to do something. One might say that the grammatical part of speech most typical of mental life is the active participle, for at every moment of time the individual is occupied in comprehending, comparing, judging, approving, disapproving, loving, hating, fearing, rejecting, yielding, adoring. The possible modes of intending are numerous, probably more numerous than the available store of present participles in our language.

It is typical of American psychology that it refused to accommodate itself to Brentano's conception of the *mental act*. What would we practical-minded people do with a merely mental act? We prefer physical acts, visible accomplishment, results. Behaviorism is more our style. The very word *act* is hard for an American to understand unless it means the moving of muscles. While Brentano would not deny the motor concomitants of mental activity, still to him the important thing is what the individual is trying to do in relating himself to the objects of his own thinking, not what he is seen externally to accomplish. The superiority of Brentano's act-psychology over behaviorism is immediately apparent in the field of religion where the subjective thrust of the mind is obviously important and where overt behavior is far less revealing.

[1] Franz Brentano. *Psychologie vom empirischen Standpunkt*, two volumes, Leipzig: Verlag Felix Meiner, 1924. (First printed in 1874.)

We need Brentano's teaching likewise to repair the otherwise static impression created by our concept of sentiment. Up to now we have dealt chiefly with the structure and attributes of sentiment, but it is its *activity* that we should emphasize. A sentiment is no mere static fitting of the mind, a simple storehouse for a cluster of related ideas and values. It is rather a mainspring of the individual's life from which radiate all manner of intentions whose purpose is to fulfill the values comprising the sentiment. At one moment a father may intend to understand something relevant to his paternal sentiment; at another moment to give comfort to the child who is the object of this sentiment; at still another time the intention may be to elicit some sign of affection from the child. Any mature sentiment is so highly differentiated that it requires a variety of intentions to express its own many-sidedness.

There is one possible misunderstanding regarding intention that must be avoided. Writing in pre-Freudian days, Brentano was perhaps insufficiently mindful of the fact that a person's goals are occasionally hidden from himself. A possessive mother may claim her intention to be the welfare of her children, though deeper exploration may show that her purposes are far more self-centered. In such a situation the motivational stream has unconscious components, and the person simply does not know his own intentions. But in such cases we are dealing with neurotic disorders where the sentiment is not mature or productive. A mature sentiment, by definition, is not at the mercy of unconscious motives that one fails to understand, but represents a style of existence that the individual has adopted after considerable reflection as a means of relating himself to life.

The goal of an intention, as Brentano pointed out, is always represented to the mind as an idea. The person intends to reach such and such an objective as conceived by himself.

If you propound me a riddle and I seek the answer, I am intending a goal that I feel to lie at the terminous of the mental act itself. Occasionally the object sought, though held in mind as an idea, conforms closely to some outward condition. Thus a century ago it was common to say, "I intend for England this spring," or "I intend for Ohio." Though we do not use the verb any longer without an auxiliary infinitive, we do frequently specify the object of our intention so clearly that its attainment can be unambiguously checked. We say, "I intend to go to England this spring," "I intend to buy a new coat," "I intend to study philosophy."

Yet many times the goal of an intention is not so clear, not even to the individual himself. Hungers and resulting strivings may be acutely felt, without one knowing precisely what will still the unrest. A youth, for instance, may be ambitious to discover a vocation, to make a name for himself, to be "somebody." But all this ardent intention is as yet unfocused. He knows not what vocation he will choose, nor to what concrete objectives he must devote himself. Sometimes we designate unrest that has not found its polarization as "divine discontent." Vividness of longing does not necessarily require clarity of object. When Thomas à Kempis wrote, "My whole desire sigheth after Thee," he was clear concerning his desire, less clear concerning the precise attributes of the Deity for whom he sighed. When the Scholastics wrote, "It is more important to love God than to know Him," they meant that the intention itself, rather than the clarity of the object, distinguishes the religious sentiment.

In developing his psychology of the act, Brentano was influenced by Catholic theology which, perceiving the vital part intention plays in the practice and rationale of religion, has given it a prominent place. Catholic writing defines intention as "an act of will, tending efficaciously to some good, proposed by the intellect as desirable and attainable." This particular definition is couched in terms of a faculty psychology, viewing will and intellect as separate departments of mental life. Dynamic psychology would prefer to avoid this duality, and say more simply that intention is the striving of an individual for a goal that is more or less clearly envisaged and congruent with a sentiment.

In Catholic theological writing concerning intention there are two points of special value for us. One is that intention is never indifferent to the means employed. To desire an end is to desire appropriate means. If a person intends health for himself he is bound to intend the means to achieve health. All our intentions require implementation, and so we conclude that any major intention, say, to seek God, will carry with it minor intentions that lead to the employment of suitable means. In other words, our special attitudes toward ritual, prayer, or matters of doctrine provide particular aids through which we carry out the more general intention of the whole sentiment. It is the differentiation of the religious sentiment that brings about this supplementary relation of intended ends and intended means.

Secondly, Catholic theology has made us aware of four grades of intention. There is psychological value in this fourfold analysis. (1) An intention is said to be *actual* when it expressly asserts the end desired. It is kept in mind while the action is taking place. If one intends to worship God and proceeds with his devotions to this end, his intention is actual. (2) An intention is *virtual* when a person has made a previous commitment, but does not feel the need for reaffirming it. Having decided to travel to Paris six months hence, I do not need to repeat the decision. Once made and not retracted, the intention is efficacious until it is carried through. A person who has decided to order his life according to a religious pattern finds this decision influencing his daily conduct even at times when he is not aware that it does so.

(3) An intention, in the Catholic sense, is *habitual* when it has never been carried out. Once made and never retracted, it has lapsed from active memory or at least it fails to instigate conduct. I say: I will take out insurance, or paint my house, or give up drinking; but I just don't get around to it. Habitual intentions, in this theological sense, seem to be those with which hell is paved. (4) Finally there are cases where intentions have not been made but we can safely infer they would have been made if the individual had been aware of the opportunity. We can assume, for example, that a good parent would intend to supply the best of vitamins for his child if he knew what they were. This grade of intention the theologians call *interpretative*, a "disposition of the will toward having an intention."[2]

The psychological value of this subtle analysis lies in its demonstration that people who maintain a religious orientation may do so in a variety of ways. In one person the "virtual" intention predominates. Such an individual, we may say, *lives* his religion though he rarely affirms it explicitly. In another, the carrying out of frequent, devotional, "actual" intentions may be the distinguishing mark. Another individual may seem to us almost "unintentionally" religious. From his behavior we feel certain he would make a religious choice if he were confronted with the issue, but this fact is only "interpretative." There are many varieties and combinations of religious intention possible for different mortals and for any one mortal at different times.

There is one final merit in the concept of intention which helps account for its importance in the psychology of religion. Its emphasis is on the future. And the future is what concerns people most of all. The chief shortcoming of American psychology up to now, I think, is its poverty in representing

[2] See "Intention" in *The Catholic Encyclopedia*, Volume 8, New York: Robert Appleton Company, 1910.

the future. While most people are absorbed in planning for, working for, dreaming for, the future, psychology for the most part is busily engaged in tracing their lives backward.[3] Most psychologists see behavior as pushed "from behind" by goads that prod us out of our past. Yet is it not characteristic of maturely directed activity, arising from the sentiments that form personality, that it is always oriented toward the future? To understand a person we have to know what he is trying to accomplish, what he is trying to become, not merely "how he got the way he is." When we look at the passengers on a railroad train they seem at first sight to be singularly aimless. But when we become acquainted with our seat mate, and learn his proposed destination and what he plans to do there, he suddenly becomes warm and human. His actions are now seen in meaningful perspective. And so it is generally: all people are in transit; and we find it less revealing to know where they came from or where they are now than to know their intended destinations.

Now many of man's intended destinations are audaciously conceived. Some people envision a One World government, they labor for it, they reach greedily for it, all the while knowing they are unlikely to achieve it in their lifetime. The poet was right: our reach exceeds our grasp. It is the reach (the long-range intention) and not the grasp (the accomplishment up to now) that confers consistency and integration on personality. Harmony of life, as Goethe said, comes not to him who attains his goals, but to him who "ceaselessly striving bestirs himself." It is the long-range intentions that have the power to order habits, thoughts, traits, into a unity of function.

[3] Cf. G. W. Allport. Geneticism versus ego-structure in theories of personality, *British Journal of Educational Psychology*, 1946, 16, 57–68; also Scientific models and human morals, *Psychological Review*, 1947, 54, 182–192.

Let me sum up. Faith is basically man's belief in the validity and attainability of some goal (value). The goal is set by desires. Desires, however, are not merely pushes from behind (drive ridden). They include such complex, future-oriented states as longing for a better world, for one's own perfection, for a completely satisfying relation to the universe. So important is this forward thrust in all desires emanating from mature sentiments that I propose the term "intention" to depict the dynamic operation we are endeavoring to describe. Better than "desire" this term designates the presence of the rational and ideational component in all productive striving. Some sort of idea of the end is always bound into the act itself. It is this inseparability of the idea of the end from the course of the striving that we call faith.

Forms of the Religious Intention

Unfortunately we cannot say that there is only one basic form of the religious intention. It is a variable phenomenon. One person may seek a beatific vision, another may long for strength to live one day in accordance with his ideals. Both intentions are religious. On one occasion the individual may be heavily concerned with some particular need—for health, for consolation, for the wisdom to make a right decision. This concern, if it touches the religious sentiment, may issue into a prayer of supplication. On another occasion the individual may desire the welfare of others, and his intention is intercessory. Feeling relief or gratitude, the intention may be one of thanksgiving. A longing to be freed from a sense of guilt leads to intentions of contrition and penance. About all we can say is that all religious acts try in some way to close the gap that exists between the actual state of one's values and the possibility of their fuller realization. The shortcoming of most definitions of religion, as I have previously said, is their tendency to center upon one limited type of religious intention. Finding release from self, perfecting one's social relations, worshiping the "wholly other," are authentic intentions, but by no means exhaust the forms that occur.

Perhaps I am being too relativistic about the matter. May there not be, after all, one central core to every religious state? A study made under the direction of Professor Braden of Northwestern University asked more than two thousand people why they were religious (if they were). Out of sixty-five suggested answers the one most commonly endorsed was that "religion gives meaning to life."[4] Should we not say, therefore, that the pursuit of meaning is the heart of religious intention? The evidence shows that this longing for meaning is indeed frequently present, but the same evidence shows that it is by no means invariably so.

Let us ask again how the religious intention differs from the philosophical. Does not the philosopher also seek the "meaning of life"? Is not his goal, too, to learn "what is permanent in the nature of things"? To be sure; but a philosopher may achieve what for him is a satisfying conception of truth without finding therein a way of life. His knowledge need not lead to action, nor affect the remainder of his life. It is only when philosophy becomes practical as well as theoretical, when it acquires the power of integrating the individual's life without remainder—intellectual, emotional, or aspirational—that it turns into religion.

It is clearly not right to confuse the religious with the philosophical intention. Love of wisdom is only one phase of the complete religious intention. Realizing this fact, Spranger attempts to identify subjective religion with the

[4] C. S. Braden. Why people are religious—a study in religious motivation, *The Journal of Bible and Religion*, 1947, 15, 38–45.

longing for unity—complete unity of thought, feeling, and deed. According to Spranger the religious intention (better to say, I think, the sum of all religious intentions) represents a desire for a total harmony, meaning thereby the individual's successive efforts to complete the incomplete, to perfect the imperfect, to conserve all values, eliminate all disvalues, to find permanence in the place of transitoriness. From this point of view the essence of the religious value can be found only in the mystical goal of oneness.[5]

We must leave this subject here. If one feels it important to seek a common denominator for all religious intentions, Spranger's solution is perhaps the best. But for my part I think we are on safer ground psychologically if we never lose sight of the individual differences that characterize the operation of the religious sentiment.

Prayer and Ritual

It is from this point of view, I think, that prayer, ritual, and dogma can best be approached. All are means of focusing the religious intention during a definite period of time. Prayer takes many forms. At one extreme it is self-reflective, analytical, hardly distinguishable from strenuous intellectual efforts to relate scattered fragments of life. Richard Cabot characterized this limiting form as follows:

We often advise each other to think it over and see what on the whole seems best; or we say, "*All things considered*, I have decided to go." Anyone who did this would be near to prayer. . . . "Considering all things" is turning from part to whole, from brilliant near-seen views, all foreground, no perspective, to a vision like that from a mountain top. Whoever tries to "see life steadily and see it whole" by retiring

[5] Eduard Spranger. *Types of Men*, Halle: Max Niemeyer Verlag, translated 1928, Part II, Chapter 6.

to a viewpoint detached from the current quotations and the latest news, has moved in the direction of prayer.[6]

More often prayer is regarded by the individual as a means of reaching a God that dwells at the terminus of the intention. Usually, too, his intention is mingled with expectation of help and response from the Object of his regard, for he would find it hard to sustain a relationship not reciprocated. Therefore God, the Object of the intention, is conceived as holding out a hand to assist the supplicant.

Yet the focusing of a religious intention through prayer does not invariably require this sense of mutuality. In at least two great religious systems, both derivatives of ancient Hinduism, no assumption is made that any supernatural powers are affected by worship or supplication. Jainism recognizes no god, but only a mechanically moral and unconscious universe. This sect believes also in twenty-four Tirthankaras or ideal beings who once lived, but have long since passed beyond the reach of the world, and are in no way affected by human prayers or offerings. Yet the ceremonies in Jaina temples are maintained with sacrifice and prayer. Intentions are reverently directed outward without thought of reciprocity. Offerings are presented to images: white rice signifies the offering of knowledge; saffron rice, of beauty. The presentation of these symbols, together with chanted verses and reflection upon the ideal for which the Tirthankara stands, bring comfort and hope, new aspirations, and strength for the moral life of the individual.[7]

In Buddhism, the story is essentially the same. The Buddhist regards Gautama as unconscious and inaccessible, and the moral universe with its principle of Karma as beyond

[6] R. C. Cabot. *What Men Live By*, Boston: Houghton Mifflin, 1914, pp. 275 f. Quoted by permission.

[7] J. B. Pratt. *The Religious Consciousness*, New York: Macmillan, 1924, p. 293.

the power of man to affect. Yet the Buddhist performs devotions that help him produce a desirable state of mind, in harmony with the moral universe. Intentions may then be directed persistently, reverently, beneficially, even though there is no actual belief in divine responsiveness. Through prayer one simply moves oneself closer to the state desired. Thus, hands *may* be held up to heaven without the expectation that hands will reach down.

Buddhist and Jainist prayers are genuine religious acts, for their intent is to relate the individual to what is central in the nature of things. In this respect they are unlike simple auto-suggestion which is a self-administered hypodermic for the purpose of achieving immediate advantage to the self without reference to an object of broader concern.

Besides prayer, ritual focuses and expresses intention. Usually ritual may be viewed as a prayer of virtual intention, running its complex course under the domination of an initial reverent idea. The symbols involved in rituals (including liturgies, hymns, religious dances) are fascinating in their origins, drawn often from feeding or death, from sex or from inebriation, with their original grossness eliminated and directed by intention toward the perfecting of the human sources from which they took their rise.

For the great majority of people the solitariness of the religious quest becomes a burden. They long to fuse their religious insights with those of their fellows under a common set of symbols. Indeed, in many cases they first learned these insights in the company of their fellows. Hence both ritual and dogma develop. The expressive symbols of ritual aid the individual by eliciting intentions that would otherwise lie mostly dormant. In psychological parlance, ritual is a form of *social facilitation* which intensifies the comparable attitudes and sentiments of all participants. At the same time dogma aims to improve and socialize the inadequate intellectual formulations of the individual. He may accept it gladly because it binds him with his fellows in a common search, and because it serves as a clarifying model to his own thought.[8] Yet, deep inside, the individual may likewise know that the meaning he derives from the dogma is not identical for him and for all believers. At best, as Whitehead points out, dogmas allow comparable experiences to be identified, while their statements are of necessity broad enough to include many varieties of individual thought. Furthermore, the dogmatic model that clarifies for one fails to clarify for another. And this is why freedom of worship in any community is essential, and why, if we prize personality at all, religious toleration is imperative.

How the Individual Validates His Faith

We come at last to the question how the religious individual justifies his faith. Even while his religious intentions are active he is incapable of cross-questioning himself. Is there a God or an orderly purpose to which he can reasonably address these intentions? It is important for him to know. How he goes about the process of validation is psychologically an interesting if complex story.

The basic phase in the process I have already described. A certain measure of confidence in the intended object is necessarily resident in every intention. Man knows his striving is real enough, and he suspects, from repeated experiences of reaching goals, that an appropriate object resides at the terminus of any persistent striving.

Is he thirsty? There is water to assuage his thirst. Is he tired? There is rest to be had. Cold? There is such a thing as warmth. Extending this reasoning to the religious striving,

[8] A. N. Whitehead. *Religion in the Making*, New York: Macmillan, 1926, p. 137.

C. S. Lewis adds: "If I find in myself a desire which no experience in this world can satisfy, the most probable explanation is that I was made for another world. If none of my earthly pleasures satisfy it, that does not prove that the universe is a fraud. Probably earthly pleasures were never *meant* to satisfy it, but only to arouse it, to suggest the real thing."[9]

Thus people find that belief is both a reflex of their striving, and on the whole a reasonable consequence to draw from the very fact of striving. A Mohammedan legend puts the matter picturesquely. A dervish was tempted by the devil to stop calling on Allah because Allah did not answer, "Here am I." The prophet Khadir appeared to the dervish in a vision with a message from Allah: "Was it not I who summoned thee to my service? Did I not make thee busy with My name? Thy calling 'Allah' was My 'Here am I.'"

According to this homily the fact of seeking is all that is required to validate the seeking.

> In that thou seekest thou hast the treasure found,
> Close with thy question is the answer bound.

One step beyond this modest validation takes us to the so-called ontological argument for the existence of God which derives the necessity of God's existence from the idea of God that man has. Although philosophers have been harsh in their rejection of the a priori statement of this proposition, an empirical or psychological version of the argument appeals to many people. Since my longing for perfect wisdom could not be the product of so finite a being as I (I would not be able to endow myself with glimpses of anything more perfect than myself), then it is inevitable for me to assume that God implanted in me the desire to know Him. The mere fact that I do undoubtedly have the idea of a perfect sovereign

---

[9] C. S. Lewis. *Christian Behaviour*, New York: Macmillan Co., 1943, pp. 57 f. Quoted by permission.

Being is a sign that the Creator has put this idea into my mind "as the mark of the workman imprinted on his work." Descartes is an ardent defender of this view. According to his reasoning, a nonentity cannot produce an entity; that which is imperfect cannot produce an idea of that which is perfect. Peter Abelard in the twelfth century expressed the same thought:

> Wish and fulfillment can severed be ne'er,
> Nor the thing prayed for come short of the prayer.

Values that cannot be achieved in this world *require* a Kingdom of Heaven.

The question may now be asked whether anyone is ever convinced by a simon-pure rational argument for the existence of God. It is certainly true that men do try to reason the matter through to a logically tight solution, just as they endeavor to find sound explanations for every riddle that confronts them. People want a rationally achieved answer. Some find it in the so-called cosmological argument which demands a sufficient first cause to explain the existence of matter, mind, and values. Yet is it not also true that unless one is awe-struck at the overpowering structure of the physical and moral universe, one could not feel the cogency of the cosmological argument? Without emotion and value he would not build a system of faith around it. Similarly, unless an individual is moved by evidences of intelligence and design in the universe, he would not take the teleological argument as support for his faith, because it would answer no lively questions for him.

What reasoning does is to lend support to a relationship that is already inherent in every sentiment—the relationship between an intention and the idea which is its object. Having first believed in the object because of the intended relationship that is set up, we normally continue to do so only if there is independent reinforcement. Sense perception and reasoning provide such support. Whenever belief receives a great deal of such reinforcement so that it conforms with sense perception, with reason, and with the beliefs of others, we are likely to call it *knowledge*. At the other extreme, when belief is deprived of all these supports, we call it *delusion*. In between these limits, where belief rests on probabilities, as the majority of beliefs do, we speak of *faith*. In all states of faith doubt is still theoretically possible though not actually dominating the mental situation at the moment.

Degrees of religious faith, as with all faith, range from high to low. Perhaps the highest is the unshakable certainty of the mystic that his immediate experience (for him the equivalent of sensory knowledge) confirms the existence of God. Perhaps the lowest degree is found in the aesthetic make-believe of Santayana who maintains that the great drama of religion would be marvelous if it were justified, so marvelous that we are entitled to act as if it were justified.

As I have previously pointed out, a relatively low degree of faith may be able to direct an enormous output of energy. One can be half-sure without being half-hearted. You and I may not have complete faith in the United Nations, but since it is our one and only hope we can and do back it with all our might. If our faith were zero we would not back it at all, but one chance in a thousand is enough for us. One recalls Descartes' reflections on this point. He remarks that a traveler who finds himself astray in some forest ought not to wander about, turning now to one side and now to another. He should walk as straight as he can in one direction, and not change it for trivial reasons. By so doing he is bound to arrive at some place probably far better than the middle of the forest.[10] Though it is not within our power to discern

---

[10] Réné Descartes. *Discourse on Method*, Part III.

certain knowledge we do well to act decisively on the basis of whatever probability attends the object of our faith.

Where does revealed religion enter into the individual's struggle for validation? It unquestionably assists him if he is persuaded that God of His free generosity has chosen to give dependable, if partial, knowledge of Himself through the devices of the intelligible universe that affect our senses, including, for example, those divinely ordained symbols employed in the sacraments which are sensible signs of what is hidden in Him. It helps to assume that God chooses to declare Himself to us in our own language.[11] Faith, based on this premise, is enjoined by the historic church, and is for millions the decisive consideration. But it is well to note that the church allows also supporting means of faith, including the rational arguments of theology, and the avenue of mystical contemplation or immediate experience. It shows psychological wisdom in multiplying the avenues through which various individuals may achieve the heightened degree of confidence in the validity of their own beliefs.

There are two final modes of validation, different in type: the mystical and the pragmatic.

Although I have no conclusive evidence on the point, I suspect that the most commonly accepted type of verification is some form of immediate experience, convincing to oneself though not as a rule to others. It is religion's peculiar secret that it brings to the individual a solemn assurance unlike anything else in life, a tranquility, an ever-present help in trouble, that makes next steps easier no matter what mesh of circumstances may entangle the life. A person who finds that the practice of faith has brought a genuine solution of conflict is convinced, for to discover order and felicity where

[11] Cf. J. Maritain. Science, Philosophy, and Faith in *Science, Philosophy and Religion: A Symposium*, New York: Conference on Science, Philosophy and Religion, 1941, Chapter 10.

there were chaos and distress is to find something extraordinarily real. This experience of a "solution found" is often attended by some degree of mystical perception. One feels that one has reached out a hand and received an answering clasp. One has sent up a cry and heard a response. Whoever verifies his faith in this manner has evidence no less convincing to him than the sensory perception which validates his beliefs in the world about him. Immediacy of this sort persuades him that revelation comes from God to man. In passing, it may be remarked that what has been called "functional revelation" seems to be more common than is "cognitive revelation." That is to say, apparently more people report an access of strength and power than claim clarifying knowledge.

Swinging abruptly to a less introverted mode of validation we wonder how many people in the present century owe their religious faith to William James's insistence that "a true thought is a thought that is an invaluable instrument of action." No need to embroil oneself in "snarling logicality" when the "will-to-believe" is available through a simple act of choice. For everyone there are higher and lower limits of attainment, and whatever leads the individual to the higher level is worth believing in. Good, believed in, finds itself embodied simply because faith changes aspiration into realization, transforms the possible into the actual. If I refuse to believe in democracy, regarding it as the dream of a fool, I shall not act democratically, and democracy will not come into being. Take the more productive option, says James. Religious faith is such an option. The core of its validation lies in the values generated and unity of life attained.

This outlook has marked appeal to action-minded individuals who have seen so many instances in life where faith in a fact (the optimistic bias) helps create the fact. Practically speaking, faith has undeniably good effects. Blending the pragmatic mode of thought with the rational one asks, "Must not that which has good effects likewise exist?" There are no effects without sufficient cause. Theism, as James himself points out, is a not infrequent accompaniment of pragmatism. Every other way of explaining value seems to break down halfway to its conclusion. The theist, for example, is persuaded that while nothing that contradicts science is likely to be true, still nothing that stops with science can be the whole truth. A more complete world view is to be achieved through affirming that the natural order is under divine rule.[12] Having committed oneself to this position the theistic-pragmatist finds his vision clarifying and his faith strengthened as he acts upon it. When, in the third chapter, I called attention to the heuristic character of mature religion I had in mind this fruitfulness of faith both for value and for understanding.

Any given individual is likely to accept several forms of validation, finding them in combination sufficient to sustain the degree of faith that he has achieved. Modes of validation do not clash; they are mutually supportive. Both reason and pragmatic sanction, for example, may blend in the individual's mind with memories of his own mystical experiences. The latter, in turn, may persuade him that divine grace is in fact available from above to help one's unbelief, and to enable one to complete the edifice of faith that no aspirant can build entirely alone.

With these many aids to verification the individual may achieve considerable certitude in the validity of his religion. Lacking, as he necessarily must, tests of absolute certainty, his own mode of validation is not necessarily convincing to others. But it may be deeply convincing to him.

[12] W. James. Reflex action and theism in *The Will to Believe and Other Essays*, New York: Longmans Green, 1897.

The Solitary Way

My theme has been the diversity of form that subjective religion assumes. Many different desires may initiate the religious quest, desires as contrasting as fear and curiosity, gratitude and conformity. Men show a varying capacity to outgrow their childhood religion, and to evolve a well-differentiated mature religious sentiment. There are many degrees in the comprehensiveness of this sentiment and in its power to integrate the life. There are different styles of doubting, different apperceptions of symbols, contrasting types of content that vary both with the culture and with the temperament and capacity of the believer. There are innumerable types of specific religious intentions. How the individual justifies his faith is a variable matter, and the certitude he achieves is his alone.

From its early beginnings to the end of the road the religious quest of the individual is solitary. Though he is socially interdependent with others in a thousand ways, yet no one else is able to provide him with the faith he evolves, nor prescribe for him his pact with the cosmos.

Often the religious sentiment is merely rudimentary in the personality, but often too it is a pervasive structure marked by the deepest sincerity. It is the portion of personality that arises at the core of the life and is directed toward the infinite. It is the region of mental life that has the longest-range intentions, and for this reason is capable of conferring marked integration upon personality, engendering meaning and peace in the face of the tragedy and confusion of life.

A man's religion is the audacious bid he makes to bind himself to creation and to the Creator. It is his ultimate attempt to enlarge and to complete his own personality by finding the supreme context in which he rightly belongs.

Index

Index